DAVID THIEL'S
power tool maintenance

Peak performance and safety for life

POPULAR WOODWORKING BOOKS

CINCINNATI, OHIO

www.popularwoodworking.com

Read This Important Safety Notice

To prevent accidents, keep safety in mind while you work. Use the safety guards installed on power equipment; they are for your protection. When working on power equipment, keep fingers away from saw blades, wear safety goggles to prevent injuries from flying wood chips and sawdust, wear hearing protectors to protect your hearing, and consider installing a dust vacuum to reduce the amount of airborne sawdust in your woodshop. Don't wear loose clothing, such as neckties or shirts with loose sleeves, or jewelry, such as rings, necklaces or bracelets, when working on power equipment. Tie back long hair to prevent it from getting caught in your equipment. People who are sensitive to certain chemicals should check the chemical content of any product before using it. The authors and editors who compiled this book have tried to make the contents as accurate and correct as possible. Plans, illustrations, photographs and text have been carefully checked. All instructions, plans and projects should be carefully read, studied and understood before beginning construction. Due to the variability of local conditions, construction materials, skill levels, etc., neither the author nor Popular Woodworking Books assumes any responsibility for any accidents, injuries, damages or other losses incurred resulting from the material presented in this book. Prices listed for supplies and equipment were current at the time of publication and are subject to change. Glass shelving should have all edges polished and must be tempered. Untempered glass shelves may shatter and can cause serious bodily injury. Tempered shelves are very strong and if they break will just crumble, minimizing personal injury.

Metric Conversion Chart

TO CONVERT	TO	MULTIPLY BY
Inches	Centimeters	2.54
Centimeters	Inches	0.4
Feet	Centimeters	30.5
Centimeters	Feet	0.03
Yards	Meters	0.9
Meters	Yards	1.1

David Thiel's Power Tool Maintenance. Copyright © 2006 by David Thiel. Printed and bound in China. All rights reserved. No part of this book may be reproduced in any form or by any electronic or mechanical means including information storage and retrieval systems without permission in writing from the publisher, except by a reviewer, who may quote brief passages in a review. Published by Popular Woodworking Books, an imprint of F&W Publications, Inc., 4700 East Galbraith Road, Cincinnati, Ohio, 45236. First edition.

Distributed in Canada by Fraser Direct
100 Armstrong Avenue
Georgetown, Ontario L7G 5S4
Canada

Distributed in the U.K. and Europe by David & Charles
Brunel House
Newton Abbot
Devon TQ12 4PU
England
Tel: (+44) 1626 323200
Fax: (+44) 1626 323319
E-mail: mail@davidandcharles.co.uk

Distributed in Australia by Capricorn Link
P.O. Box 704
Windsor, NSW 2756
Australia

Visit our Web site at www.popularwoodworking.com for information on more resources for woodworkers.

Other fine Popular Woodworking Books are available from your local bookstore or direct from the publisher.

10   09   08   07   06   5   4   3   2   1

Library of Congress Cataloging-in-Publication Data

Thiel, David, 1962-
    David Thiel's power tool maintenance / David Thiel.
      p.   cm.
    Includes index.
    ISBN-13: 978-1-55870-755-9 (pbk.: alk. paper)
    ISBN-10: 1-55870-755-7 (pbk.: alk. paper)
    ISBN-13: 978-1-55870-767-2 (hardcover: alk. paper)
    ISBN-10: 1-55870-767-0 (hardcover: alk. paper)
    1. Woodworking tools—Maintenance and repair.
        I. Title: Power tool maintenance.   II. Title.
TT186.T42   2006
684'.083—dc22   2005023253

ACQUISITIONS EDITOR: Jim Stack
EDITOR: Amy Hattersley
DESIGNER: Brian Roeth
PAGE LAYOUT: Dragonfly Graphics, L.L.C.
ILLUSTRATOR: Mary Jane Favorite
PRODUCTION COORDINATOR: Jennifer L. Wagner

fw
F+W PUBLICATIONS, INC.

This book is dedicated to my father, Klaus, who came to America from his native Germany with his Lehrbrief in his hand proclaiming him a woodworker. His guidance gave me the interest and opportunity to learn about woodworking and the tools and machines that make this wonderful skill possible. Thanks, Dad.

About the Author

David Thiel is a senior editor for *Popular Woodworking* magazine and has been with the publication since 1994. His primary responsibility has been to test and review new woodworking tools and products, both individually and in group reviews. Although he knows about hand tools as well, he still prefers a tool with a tail. He is the Tool Guy, but he still enjoys building projects and writing other non-tool-related articles for the magazine.

David is also the host of the DIY Network television show, *Tools & Techniques*, which focuses on improving the viewer's knowledge about a wide range of tools and their proper use.

Acknowledgements

I'd like to thank the many woodworking tool manufacturers I've known over the years for recognizing the necessary balance between reviewing a tool honestly and still being able to discuss things in a friendly manner. I count many product managers, marketing managers and public relations professionals among my friends. Thank you for all your timely help over the years … you know who you are.

I also want to thank the rest of the *Popular Woodworking* staff for putting up with me every time a new tool shows up in the office and I have to try and get everyone else as excited about the new arrival as I am. Thanks for your patience.

contents

Welcome. This book is a direct response to the many, many articles and books already in print regarding the same topic: woodworking power tool maintenance. No, the world really doesn't need another one, but it does need a book on tool maintenance that makes sense. It seems that authorities on the subject are in constant battle with one another to make it more difficult to use our tools, and in the process they're teaching every woodworker that he should be spending as much time maintaining his tools as he is working wood.

Not this one. The joy of woodworking should be in doing the woodworking. And, as shocking as it sounds, it's not necessary to strip down and regrease the gears on your table saw before you start every project. In fact, you shouldn't even be losing sleep over the information that your table saw's top is out of flat by .0001" (0.0025mm) in one corner.

I read a book a number of years ago about making your own beer at home. Whenever the author got to a part that seemed slightly tricky, his suggestion was, "Relax, have a home brew!" Well, I'm not going to tell you to grab a beer, but I will suggest that when you get the urge to re-

intro

introduction

wind the motor on your trim router because it's over two years old, you should "Relax and cut some wood."

This book includes ten chapters on the most common power tools that woodworkers use in their shops. It's not all-inclusive and there are going to be things you'll encounter on your tools and machines that aren't addressed in this book. But it will give you the basic building blocks to keep your tools working well for you — well enough that you'll be able to spend your time as a woodworker, not a machinist.

I've also given you my unvarnished opinion about some tools and some of the features that are now common on these tools. These are my opinions and there are bound to be readers (and manufacturers) that don't agree with me. But after 25 years as a woodworker and 10 as a tool reviewer, I kind of feel like I'm entitled to my opinion.

I hope this book proves useful and entertaining to you and ultimately helps you with your passion — woodworking.

David Thiel

table saws

THE TABLE SAW IS THE MOST USEFUL TOOL in your shop. Strangely enough, the British seem to think it's the band saw. They're wrong. Well, yes, you should own a band saw as well, but the table saw is the workhorse in any woodworking shop. For sheet goods (plywood, MDF, melamine) and for solid lumber it's the tool that rips and crosscuts all your material straight, square and effortlessly — assuming you've got it tuned properly and that you're using it correctly.

The origin of the table saw is slightly fuzzy. The most colorful story is that of Sister Tabitha Babbitt (circa 1784-1854) of the Harvard Shaker community in Massachusetts. The story is that she was watching some of the brothers use a two-man pit saw, and it appeared to her that the back-and-forth motion was particularly wasteful of their energy. Her work for the community involved working at a spinning wheel, and she made a mental leap to add a circular blade to a spinning wheel mechanism. According to historical records, this "enlightenment" took place around 1810.

Unfortunately for Sister Tabitha, a number of other stories credit the use of a circular saw blade in Holland in the mid 18th century. In addition, a fellow by the name of Samuel Miller from Southampton, England, was granted a patent for a circular saw in either 1777 or 1779. All versions are possible and certainly could have happened. Regardless, the use of a metal disc with cutting teeth did revolutionize woodworking and continues to be an important machine for today's woodworkers.

Not having had the pleasure of ever meeting you, I don't know if you are just starting in woodworking or have been making dust for years. If you're just starting, I'm just in time — the first machine to buy is a table saw, and I'm going to help you decide which one you need. If you already have a table saw, I hope I can confirm that you indeed do have the correct one or give you lots of ammo to upgrade. But mostly I'll talk about how to tune it up the first time — and every time — and how you can accessorize to get the most from your saw.

Parts and Types

Today's table saw breaks down into five parts. A circular saw blade is mounted on a spinning shaft that is attached to a motor by a single or series of drive belts. The blade extends through a slot in a tabletop and is raised, lowered and beveled using shafts with worm gears that mesh with pivot arms. The table surface has a locking fence mounted arallel to the blade that is used to guide the wood through the spinning blade. Those are the basics, and each of these parts can be different depending on the type of table saw. So let's take a look at the categories of table saws.

There are essentially four categories of table saws for woodworkers to consider (excluding industrial saws). As of just a few years ago there were only three. That's what we call progress, and it's not a bad thing at all. The four categories are benchtop, contractor, cabinet and hybrid saws.

Benchtop saws are exactly what they sound like: They are saws able to be used on your bench top. They are lightweight, extremely portable and the best buddy of many a contractor. They can be tossed in the back of a pickup truck and taken to a job site very easily. Once on site they can be quickly clamped to a set of planks and horses; many come with their own fold-away stands. This portability also makes these saws very handy for space-challenged home woodworkers. They can be tucked away under a bench or in a corner when not in use. Most of these saws are reasonably inexpensive, ranging in price between $100 and $500. For a just-starting woodworker this price can be very attractive.

But benchtop saws are not always the right selection. Though they're inexpensive and portable, there are trade-offs. Benchtop table saws are powered by universal motors. These are the same types of motors that power your router or circular saw. While capable of doing the job, these motors are actually designed for providing short bursts of speed and don't have as much torque as an induction motor. This means that you may be capable of ripping a $2\frac{1}{2}$" (64mm) thick piece of white oak on your benchtop saw, but it's likely to be slow going, and you won't be able to do this over and over without putting a serious strain on the motor.

Another limitation on benchtop saws is capacity. Because they're small and portable, it's difficult to rip a longer board without running into concerns of tipping. This can be avoided by adding outfeed rollers or tables. If it's not lumber but sheet goods (like a sheet of $^3/4$" [19mm] plywood), these smaller saws just aren't big enough to support the sheet during the cut. You're just as well off going back to your circular saw and an edge guide. Most benchtop saws' top surface, or table, is made of lightweight aluminum. Again, although this is a benefit for portability, it's a limitation as far as stability. These tops are more prone to flexing under weight and that can affect the quality of the cut.

Also less than perfect are the rip fences and miter guides on benchtop saws. Both of these features are important considerations when shopping for any table saw. The rip fence must lock down solidly and in parallel with the blade or your cut quality can be affected — and it can be dangerous. The fences on benchtop saws are lightweight and often have problems locking adequately and in parallel — okay for some contractor work but not for most woodworking. The miter gauges are a concern with all table saws, but the standard equipment for benchtop saws is even less useful.

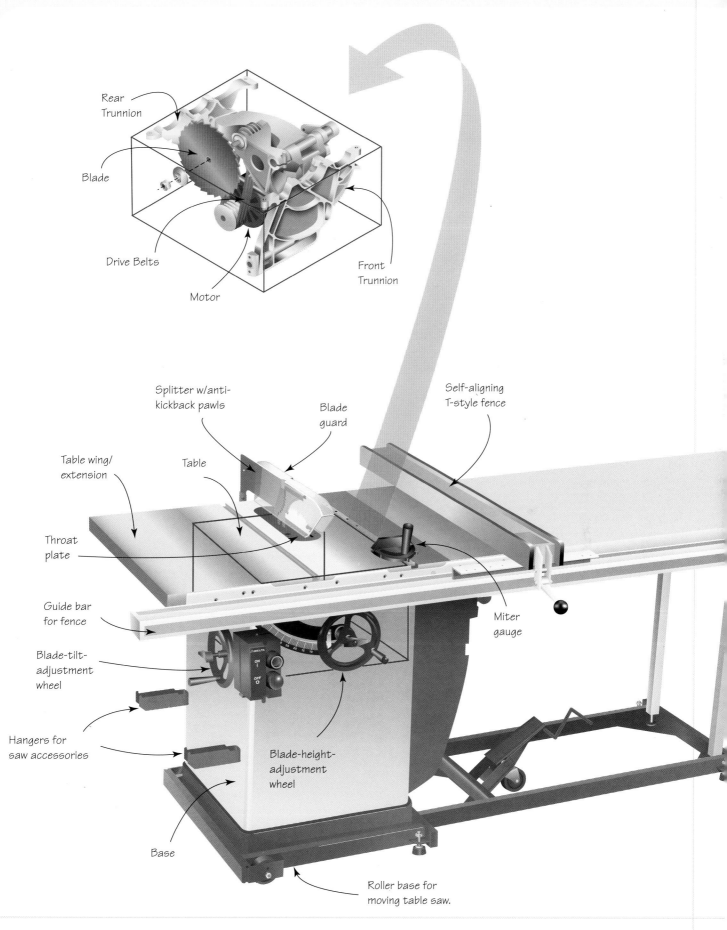

Rear Trunnion

Blade

Drive Belts

Motor

Front Trunnion

Splitter w/anti-kickback pawls

Blade guard

Self-aligning T-style fence

Table wing/ extension

Table

Throat plate

Guide bar for fence

Blade-tilt-adjustment wheel

Hangers for saw accessories

Miter gauge

Blade-height-adjustment wheel

Base

Roller base for moving table saw.

Contractor saws are probably the most common table saws in woodworking shops. They offer a good balance between capacity, power and affordability. Contractor saws most often include an open-frame metal stand to support the saw. The main table surface of contractor saws is usually cast iron, but the wings (the table extensions to either side of the main table) can vary from aluminum to open, waffle-patterned cast iron and, preferably, solid cast-iron wings. I prefer the solid cast-iron wings because they offer a flat, stable work surface and add weight to the saw that helps to reduce vibration. Though the weight of the open-design wings is decent, I've pinched too many fingers and dropped too many pencils through the holes to be happy with this design.

Contractor saws also offer one significant step up from benchtop saws — an induction motor. These motors are designed for continuous use and provide reliable and increased torque when cutting lumber. The motors on contractor saws are suspended behind the body and are connected to the motor by a belt(s). This configuration allows the suspended weight of the motor itself to provide the belt tension to spin the blade — simple and logical. However, the motor extending out the back of the saw, and the fact that the motor must be able to swing sideways to adjust the bevel angle, makes it difficult to enclose the saw box for dust collection. It's also been documented that because of the rear-mounted motor's lighter weight trunnions, some trunnion assemblies can twist slightly when the blade is angled for bevel cuts. This can pull the blade out of parallel with the rip fence causing burning on the wood or inaccuracies in the cut.

Overall, the contractor saw is a good machine for most woodwork-

ers. A fine blend of capability and affordability (between $350 and $800 — check price). One word of caution: Some manufacturers will put together a saw model that looks very much like a contractor saw, with stand, improved table and fence, but the motor is still a universal motor. These are often priced very attractively, but with the universal motor, they're not really a contractor saw. They're dressed-up benchtop saws. Check the motor!

Cabinet saws are the granddaddy of table saws. While contractor saws usually have an open-frame stand, cabinet saws have (drum roll, please) a cabinet! The cabinet adds some extra weight and stability to the saw, and it makes dust collection hookup much more efficient. But cabinet saws are a step up for more reasons than their stand. Many cabinet saws are powered by 220-volt induction motors rated at three or five horsepower. That's a real advantage. The move up to induction motors is good, but a larger motor makes it possible to cruise through 3" (76mm) hard maple in a rip cut without slowing down significantly.

Beyond the motor, cabinet saws are also different below the table. On a contractor saw the trunnions and blade assembly are suspended from the saw's tabletop (because there really isn't much frame on the saw to attach anything to). This setup is economical, but it makes it harder to adjust the relationship of the blade to the table to keep cuts straight. A cabinet saw has the trunnions and motor assembly mounted to the cabinet. This leaves the top floating free and makes it easier to adjust the blade orientation. This arrangement also helps move the vibration of the running saw away from the table (where you're working and resting your wood) and transfers it to the cabinet. Therefore, cabinet saws are smoother running with less vibration.

Cabinet saws also traditionally offer better capacity for cutting, offering larger tabletops and extended side tables. Being heavy machines, cabinet saws are usually set in place in a shop and not moved. However, because the 21st-century woodworker is often space challenged, mobile bases that allow mobility and stability are becoming a standard feature.

Hybrid saws are another group of saws that aren't exactly what they seem. Everybody wants a cabinet saw (for the reasons given previously), but they frequently can't afford a $1,500 saw, or they may not have a shop outfitted for 220 power. So manufacturers started putting together saws that had either partially enclosed bases or actual enclosed cabinets. Although the motor remained a smaller induction style (under 2 horsepower) 110-volt model, it was repositioned from the back of the saw and moved inside. This move did two clever things: It improved the ability to add efficient dust collection, and because the still-suspended motor is now hanging straight down from the blade, it reduced the concern of blade twist when tilted for bevel cuts. This is a good change.

Hybrid saws offer better fence systems and larger table surfaces. All these things make them attractive and a good alternative to contractor saws. But the buyer (that's you) needs to be aware that the hybrid saw is a tricked-out contractor saw, not a cabinet saw. As long as you know that, the hybrid saw can be a nice addition to your shop.

Location, Location, Location

Now that we know something about table saws, let's talk about what kind of living space they need. Naturally, the type of saw will determine if it has a permanent or transient home in your shop. In either case, there are some size issues to deal with. The types of wood you will be cutting on your table saw come in two general sizes. Hardwood averages about 8" (203mm) wide by 96" (2438mm) long. Plywood is 48" × 96" (1219mm × 2438mm). Either can be ripped or crosscut on a table saw. So, when you consider those relationships, you find out how much clear space must be left around your table saw to handle all the possible cuts.

The illustration on this page shows that you essentially need eight feet of clear space to the infeed and outfeed sides of the table saw as well as eight feet to the left of the blade. That's a pretty serious allocation of space in a tight workshop. It's also the most space you will have to allocate for any one woodworking machine, so it's a good idea to decide where your table saw goes first, then fill in the rest of the machines after that.

Another important factor in location is where the saw is located in reference to your materials and the other machines. Because the table saw is often where larger wood is made smaller, it should usually be located near your lumber storage so you don't have to carry anything too far. It's also smart to locate it near your planer and jointer (for the same reasons), and having these three machines near each other makes joint dust collection much more possible.

Setup

So let's assume you've picked out the perfect table saw for you and you have its new home all ready for it. That would mean you have the appropriate power run to the saw's location, and you've made some consideration for dust collection — more on the latter

later. Later, latter? Whatever.

Now, if you picked up a contractor saw at the local Home Depot, you had to get it home and get it in your shop. They're not light, so hopefully you had the help of at least one friend. If you happened to have ordered a cabinet saw by catalog or on the Internet, you might be unpleasantly surprised when it arrives on your doorstep. Actually, when it arrives at the end of your drive. It's your responsibility to get it off the truck. Cabinet saws are heavier than contractor saws and are usually packed in one crate rather than a few lighter

pieces. If you're lucky, the truck will have a lift gate. If not, I hope you have some really good friends. The moral? Check with your retailer as to what type of delivery you can expect on your new toy so you won't be surprised.

Once it's in your shop, unpack everything and read through the instructions. No, really — read through the instructions. It's mostly to find out if all the parts are there, because it's really annoying to discover you need to attach the dust port before you attach the saw to the base. It's worth a look, and I won't tell any of your buddies

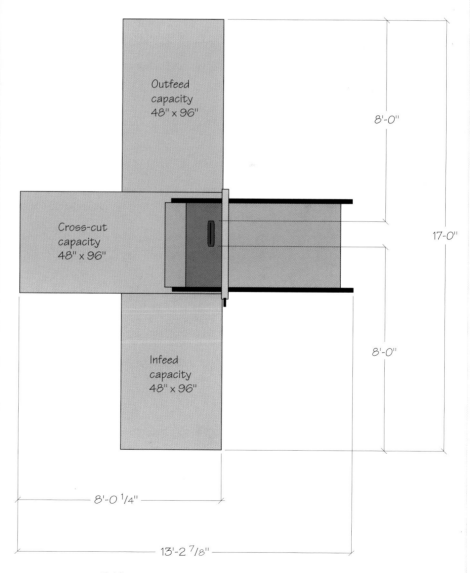

Table saw space requirements

you cheated.

Every saw's setup is slightly different, so follow the instructions to get the basics managed. Then follow the steps and photos on the following pages to check for the alignments and setups that will get you running true and smooth.

The Motor: Whether you had to attach the motor to the mounting brackets or it was already assembled, to ensure that it's running smoothly and with the least amount of vibration, the pulleys need to be in alignment with one another. This isn't too complicated a concept, but it can be tricky to get into the right position to check the alignment. And, even harder to work all the adjustments at once. A

36" (914mm) steel rule will be your best friend in this step. By laying the rule across the motor and blade pulleys you'll be able to tell not only if they're in alignment but also if either is cocked, which will tend to let the belt wander. Your rule should lay flat on both sides of each of the pulleys. If this isn't the case, adjust the motor mount bolts and, if necessary, slide the pulley in or out on the shaft, remembering to retighten the pulley. There's a long story there, but let's just say the horrible noise only lasted for a few minutes. Oops.

The Table: If you've attached the wings as instructed, they should be flush to the main (center) table. It's possible they won't automatically be

flush the entire depth of the top. But if you start at the front of the saw, tighten the first bolt and work your way back, you can actually get a little flex out of the top to match the full depth. Don't sweat it; steel moves just like wood. Okay, it's time to dispel a cliché. Although it's really nice to have a perfectly flat saw top, if it's within a few .001" (.03mm) it's okay! It's not a reference table, it's a table saw. Get your 36" (914mm) steel rule out again, and lay it from corner to corner, front to back and side to side on the top. If you can't see light you're in good shape. If you get out your feeler gauges, you need to chill out!

The Blade: Okay, this part should be pretty dead on. The blade needs to

Place a steel rule against the outer face of both pulleys (the interior pulley can't be seen here, but it can be felt). You will notice a good contractor saw upgrade in the linkbelt, instead of a standard V-belt. (The linkbelts reduce vibration.) You might also notice the amount of dust built up on the belt. One more place to clean!

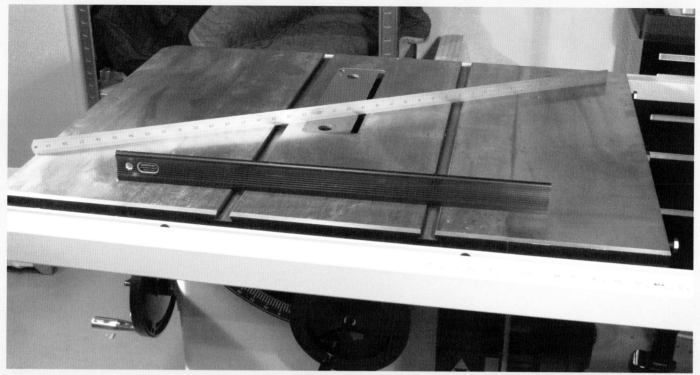

Whether you're using a simple steel straightedge or a more expensive straightedge (front), you should be able to check in any direction on the top and still see no significant gap. A light shone behind the straightedge will make any gap much more obvious. Dead perfect is wonderful, but if you have a gap less than 1⁄32" (0.8mm) you're still okay.

be perfectly parallel to the miter slots (those steel valleys running on either side of the blade). They should already be perfectly parallel to one another; if not, your top is screwed up and you should send it back. More likely than not your blade will be parallel to the miter slots, because this is one of those important quality assurance checks that happen at the factory before they let the saw out the door. But, shipping and delivery…who knows. So, get a rule (a 6" [152mm] steel rule will work … sensing a trend?) and measure from the left side of a tooth at the front of the blade (saw unplugged, please) to the miter slot on the left. Then, keeping track of the same front tooth (the blade's, not yours), rotate the blade to the rear on the saw and measure the distance between the miter slot and blade at that location. They should be the same. If they're not (and again, be realistic about measuring — 1⁄64" [0.4mm] off may be worth correct-

ing. Less than that, no.), you'll need to adjust the top in relation to the trunnions. This is different on a cabinet saw and a contractor saw. Read the instructions, or check with the manufacturer. It's slightly different on every saw.

Okay, one more blade check. The blade should be a perfect 90° in relationship to the table saw top. A steel engineer's square is great for checking this. Run the blade angle over to the full 90° position, and place the square against the blade body, not one of the teeth. If it's not perfect, there's a bolt that serves as a stop for the beveling mechanism (not always the same on each saw, but pretty darn close). Back off the jamb nut and adjust the stop bolt until you're at 90°. Now, while you're crawling around under the saw, you should check the stop for the 45° position as well. Your engineer's square won't work here, but a simple drafting square or any number of high-tech tools can help you out.

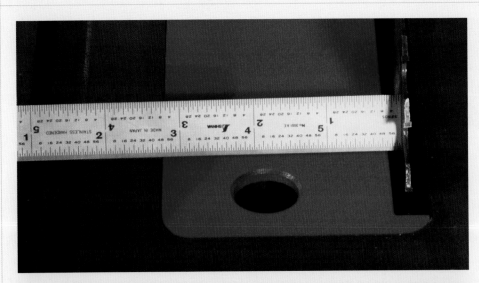

The first step is to make sure the miter slots in the table align correctly with the trunnions and the blade. Simply measure from the blade body to the slot at the front of the blade. If a steel rule seems too imprecise for you, there are dial indicators that can be used to measure this setup to .001" (0.025mm). Fun, but a little over the top.

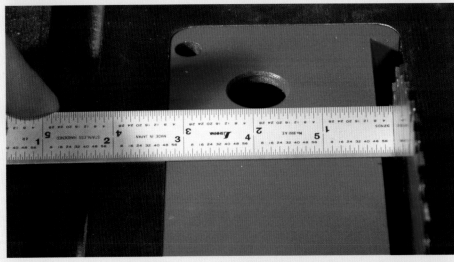

The second step is to rotate the blade and measure from the same blade location at the rear of the blade opening. Both measurements should be very close.

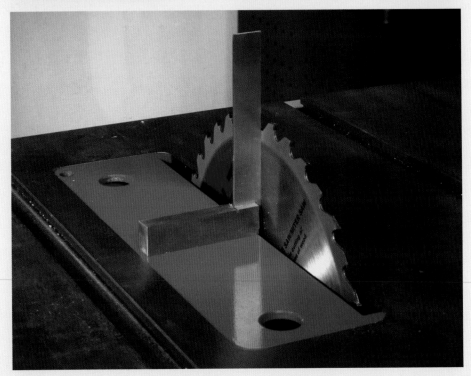

An engineer's square placed evenly between the tabletop and blade body will show no gap against the blade when at a perfect 90°.

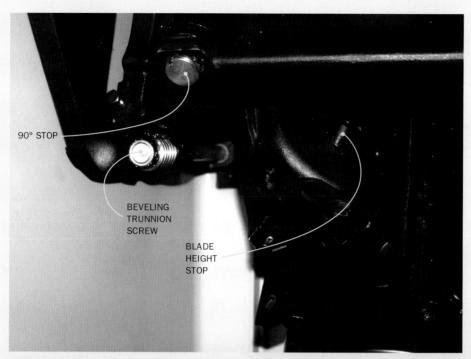

90° STOP

BEVELING
TRUNNION
SCREW

BLADE
HEIGHT
STOP

This is a pretty good look at two of the stops on the saw. At left is the 90° stop for the blade bevel. On the opposite side of the saw (shyly away from the camera) is a similar stop for the 45° adjustment. Directly below the 90° stop is the beveling trunnion screw. Also visible in the middle of the photo is the blade height stop, which is another good one to know about, though not discussed in the main text. It's not usually one you need to adjust, but if the blade mechanism rises too far toward the table, a bad noise will be heard.

Another very useful (but more expensive) way to check for accurate blade alignment is with a tool like this. The magnetic base holds the tool tightly to the saw table. When the blade is brought to 90° or 45°, the light indicates a perfect contact and an accurate saw. Cool, fun but still slightly pricey. Ask for it for your birthday.

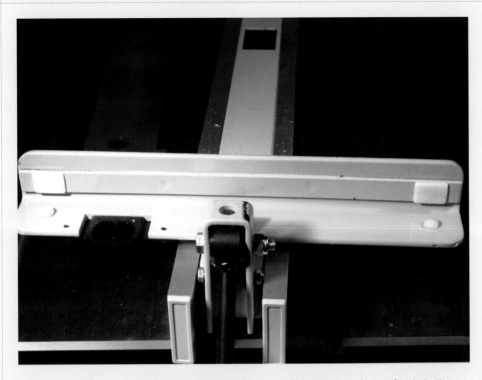

The better table saw fences can be adjusted for toe (left-to-right), to be perfectly in line with the blade, as well as for a perfect right angle to the saw table. The fence shown here has both adjustments easily accessible. The two round pads on either side of the fence are for adjusting to 90° to the table and can be reached easily from the top side of the fence, with the fence in place. The rectangular pads are used to adjust for toe; unfortunately, the fence needs to be removed to make these adjustments.

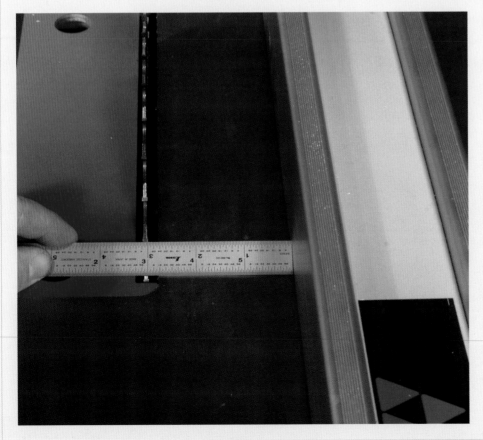

As with aligning the blade to the miter slots, the fence adjustment is checked at both the front and back of the blade. It's easier to make this check if you adjust the fence to a readily identified distance from the blade, such as the 3" (76mm) shown here.

The Fence: The last truly important setting to check is the fence. The fence face that the material runs against needs to be perpendicular (90°) to the saw table, and the entire fence needs to be parallel to the blade. We don't have to worry whether it's parallel to the miter slots because you already checked their relationship to the blade, right? Start with perpendicular using your engineer's square. The trick here is if the fence face is out of square you might have to do some unorthodox adjusting. Not all fences are designed to allow adjustment for perpendicular. Check your manual (again, all fences are slightly different). If there's no adjustment, you may need to use some strips of masking tape behind the fence face to shim it to square. With luck, your manual will show a simple adjustment.

The same method you used to check the parallelism between the blade and miter slot is used to check the fence parallelism. Again, if it's out more than a 1/64" (0.4mm) it's worth fixing. And most fences offer a method for this adjustment without masking tape. Check your manual.

How To

There are dozens and dozens of books available on how to use a table saw. This isn't one of them. I will give you a couple of comments on their usage that relate to safety and maintenance, but for how to cut a dado, you'll have to look elsewhere.

The table saw is frequently identified as the most dangerous machine in a woodworking shop. Yes, it can be dangerous, but it's my strong belief that this "dangerous" reputation is mostly due to the fact that table saws are the most common and most used machines in a woodworking shop. So, there are lots more chances for accidents. But that doesn't mean you shouldn't think and work safely every time you use one. These safety steps aren't that crazy and will make your work much safer.

1. Use a guard whenever you can (some table saw operations require the guard be removed). If your current guard is annoying and inconvenient, buy a better one.

2. Use a zero-clearance throat insert. Most table saws aren't sold with one, but by adding this simple accessory you'll avoid trapped waste pieces and lots of headaches.

3. Use a push stick for any piece smaller than 6" (152mm) wide. It's that simple. Find a style you like and keep it right on your fence. It doesn't have to be fancy, and don't worry if it gets cut up. You can always make a new push stick. Fingers grow back much slower!

4. Keep your saw neat and uncluttered. Not only is this a good work practice but trying to move things out of the way while you're using the saw is just plain dangerous.

5. Keep the saw tuned and aligned. Many of the mistakes that happen on table saws are due to boards pinched between the fence and blade. It's all about the alignment. Check your saw before each project.

6. When you're using the saw, never stand directly behind the blade. This is the kickback zone, and you will get hurt, eventually, if you don't pay attention to this area.

Maintenance

I've already talked about the basic set-up concerns. Each of these alignment steps (except for aligning the pulleys) is something that should be rechecked periodically. You don't have to post a maintenance schedule next to your tool (though some folks will, and that's okay, but there are 12-step programs available). Better if you take the time to check your saw before each new woodworking project. That's a reasonable maintenance schedule.

Along with alignment, I strongly recommend a good cleaning before each project. You should already have your saw hooked up to some type of dust collection, but that doesn't take care of everything. Let me add a couple of comments about dust collection here. You can use a central shop system that will do a wonderful job, or you can hook up a simple two-bag portable unit (as shown below) right next to your saw. Either way, do use dust collection. It makes the saw easier to use (no dust thrown up in the air obscuring your vision), and it will keep the machine running better. Dust gets into gears and crevices. Keeping most of the dust out of the air initially will make maintenance easier.

So, cleaning… get out your shop vacuum and crawl under the saw (unplug, please). No, it's not fun or comfortable, but you need to suck out the trunnion area (see photo on the next page). This is where dust will accumulate and gum up the gears. You also should get the dust out from around the blade shroud. Waste pieces

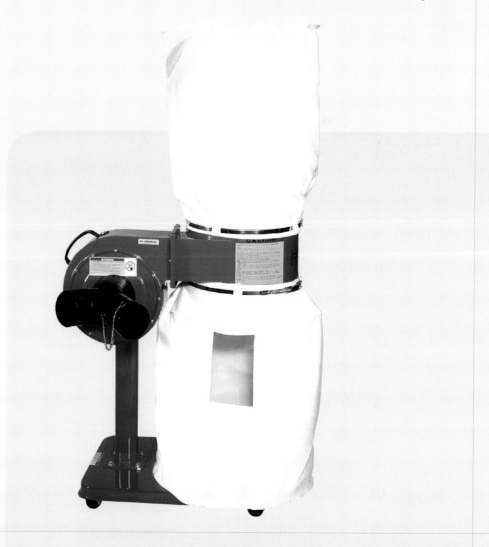

This is a good look at the wood dust that can build up on the interior surfaces of a saw. That's the rear trunnion coated with mahogany dust. I don't think it's too hard to imagine how that might affect smooth beveling of the blade.

As mentioned in the text, even though you have a dust collector hooked up, it doesn't mean it's working perfectly. This cabinet saw is hooked up to an automatic dust collection system, but dust still manages to build up inside. Make sure the dust port isn't obscured. This will keep things cleaner, easier.

are known to hang around here and eventually can get kicked back up by the blade. This can be either dangerous or just scary. You don't need an unexplained BANG while you're using your saw — it'll send you out to change your shorts. Get the dust out from under the throat plate as well. If there's dust there it won't sit flat and can cause your workpiece to hang up. And clean up any debris from around the dust collection port. It doesn't take much to reduce the draw through that port, then you'll be cleaning lots of dust out from under the saw with a dust pan. Get the dust out of the miter gauge slots and don't overlook the fence guide rails. These are places where critical alignment and easy movement are important. Dust will screw that up quickly.

With everything nice and tidy, it's time to make them slippery. The gears don't need greasing every time you clean, but periodic greasing will make things operate much smoother. There are two sets of toothed gears under the saw that you want to keep sliding easily. One set is a lead screw and gears that adjust the height of the blade. The other is a pair of half-moon gears that adjust the blade angle. Both need greasing. Now, let's talk about "greasing." Traditionally actual grease is fine for this application and you can still use it. However, technology advances and it's good to look at some options. Standard grease is prone to collect dust. Over time this will sludge the grease and add grit to the motion. To avoid this, there are a couple of options to consider. Lithium grease (a spray-on lubricant that gets into the nooks and crannies better than standard grease) and other specially formulated spray lubricants are reasonable options. The decision is yours, but regardless, make it slide.

Just two more maintenance details and you're ready to rip. The table saw top needs to be in good shape as well. This is actually a more routine maintenance step than any of the others.

Because it's important that your wood move past the blade with nothing to interrupt it (for safety and most efficient function) the tabletop should be slightly lubricated as well. But you don't want any type of lubricant that might stay on the wood and adversely affect a finish on your project. The tried and true method is to use paraffin, or simple canning wax, that you can buy at your grocery store. This dry wax can be rubbed quickly across the metal (and other) surfaces of the saw that will have wood rubbing against them. This includes the fence face. There are also some spray lubricants available that can be simply sprayed on the surfaces. Just make sure they aren't silicon sprays. These can cause fisheye in your finish if allowed to stay on the wood surface.

And last, make sure you've got a sharp blade on your saw. Dull blades are inefficient and dangerous. If you feel like you're pushing harder than you should to make a cut, the first thing to consider should be a dull blade. Also, while half of you probably put a combination saw blade (one designed to rip and crosscut) on your saw and leave it alone, I'd encourage you to consider dedicated function blades (see "Using the Correct Saw Blade"). A rip blade rips wood better and cleaner than a combination blade. A dedicated crosscut blade is also much better at that single task than a combination blade. Yes, it costs more, but it's better woodworking.

Two examples of the many options for keeping your saw's works sliding easily. The white lithium grease at left performs much as a standard grease but is an aerosol spray so the grease penetrates into the toughest locations. The lubricant at right is similar; both should be used with adequate ventilation. Take note of the thin applicator wand. This gets the lubricant into the smallest of locations with little difficulty.

From high-tech sprays to low-tech canning wax, these are just a few of the ways to make your saw top frictionless enough to ease work past the saw blade. While the paraffin (wax) will provide a good surface and some protection against rust, other products are formulated to first remove any surface rust (TopSaver) Then you should follow up with a sealant and lubricant (TopCote).

Accessories

I've touched on a couple of accessories already that I think are necessary. Zero-clearance plates and push sticks are the two main accessories mentioned. Get (or make) more than one of each. Both are disposable items that will get cut up in use.

Right along with your push stick, you need a pair of safety glasses that are comfortable for you (so you'll use them). Keep them right near the "on" switch of your saw. I'd also recommend hearing protection of some type. Although the saw may not sound amazingly loud, it's the pitch of sound made by the blade that will ultimately affect your hearing. Better to be safe.

You should also use a blade guard, as mentioned, and you may also benefit from an independent splitter. Along with these items, another item that you can make or purchase is a featherboard. This is used to hold material down to the saw table and against the fence during the operation. Featherboards (shown at right) are jigs that have stiff bristles, or feathers that are angled to allow the wood to pass them (flexing and applying pressure) but won't allow the wood to be moved in the opposite direction easily. These are great accessories to reduce kickback concerns on your saw.

No matter what size saw you're using, there will be a time when what you're cutting won't fit completely on the saw. Having some type of roller stand or outfeed table to support work on the far side and left side of the saw can save your back and provide a much safer working experience.

Shown are a few good accessories to consider: home-made push stick, a zero-clearance throat insert, an upgraded miter gauge, an independent splitter with anti-kickback teeth, a splitter with an attached blade guard (at the top of the photo), and, if you're using a contractor saw, a linkbelt can quickly smooth out the ride.

PHOTO BY AL PARRISH

Using the Correct Saw Blade

When using a table saw (or even a miter saw) using the correct saw blade will improve the saw's performance and the quality of the cut. Most woodworkers will use three types of saw blades. (At least they *should* use three blades.) Many simply put a combination blade on the saw and leave it at that. Not what I would recommend.

A combination saw blade is aptly named because it can be used for crosscutting (across the grain direction) or for ripping (cutting with the grain direction). Actually, any blade can be used for both of these tasks, but not as efficiently as one designed for that purpose. So though the combination blade can be used for both ripping and crosscutting, it's a compromise and less efficient at both.

There are two types of teeth to pay attention to on saw blades. One is a raker tooth that has a flat top. The other is a bevel-top tooth that comes to a point. On a blade designed for ripping the teeth are all of the raker design. Because the cut is happening with the grain, the raker tooth can efficiently and cleanly split the wood.

When cutting across the grain a raker tooth would tear the wood badly, leaving a very unattractive edge and back face. The more appropriate bevel-top tooth is designed to slice through the wood fibers, reducing the tear-out and

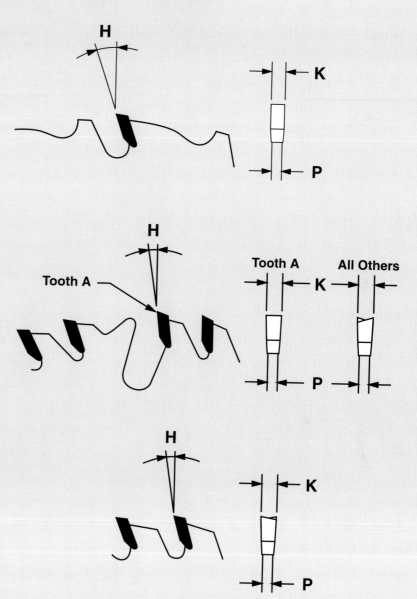

cutting more efficiently. And because the blade is cutting a kerf with two sides, the slicing action needs to take place on both sides of the blade. That's why blades designed for crosscutting have these slicing teeth oriented in a staggered left-right-left pattern. This is called an alternate top bevel tooth design.

So what's a combination

blade? Just what it sounds like. A combination blade will most often have four alternating bevel-top teeth grouped together (left-right-left-right) with a flat raker tooth leading them into the cut. This isn't a bad blade, but there are compromises being made and you'll have to decide how significant the difference will be to your woodworking.

ART COMPLIMENTS
OF FREUD

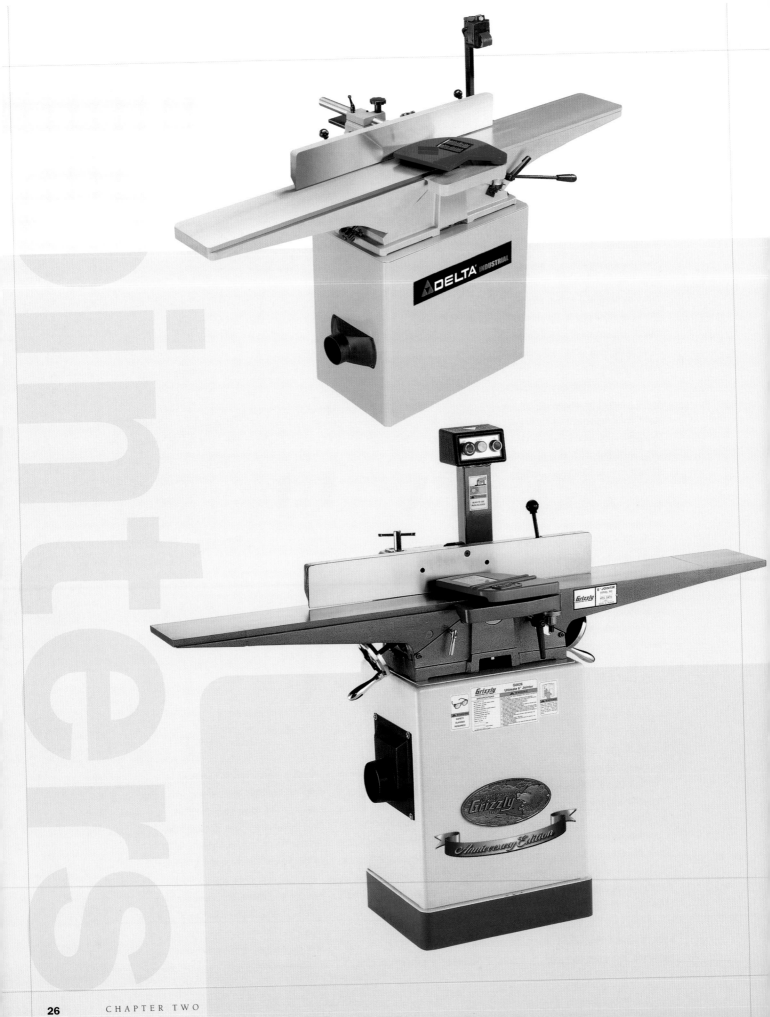

jointers

JOINTERS ARE HALF OF THE dynamic duo of jointers and planers that make flat, straight, accurately dimensioned lumber a possibility. Although they can be used independently for a number of woodworking operations, their true strength is as part of this woodworking team.

Most commonly jointers are used to true and straighten boards before they are run to their finished thickness in a planer. Though a planer just slices the material from the board without much operator input, a jointer requires a bit of technique to get the board ready for the planer.

You should use the jointer to straighten and flatten one face and one edge of the board. I start with a face (round side up) and make light passes without putting too much pressure on the board. When the jointer is taking cuts fully across the width of the board and along the full length, the face is flat.

To square the board, you want to joint one edge of the board straight and square to the face you just surfaced. Use the same light passes on the edge with the recently flattened face referencing against the fence. That's all there is to it!

A jointer consists of two metal tables on either side of a rotating set of blades. The blades are set in a cutterhead and can number two, three or four. The knives are adjusted so that the tops of the knives are set at exactly the same height as the outfeed table surface. The infeed table is adjustable, up and down, and this is what makes the jointer work. As a board is fed over the infeed table and into the cutterhead, the head removes an amount of wood equal to the offset of the infeed table to the knives.

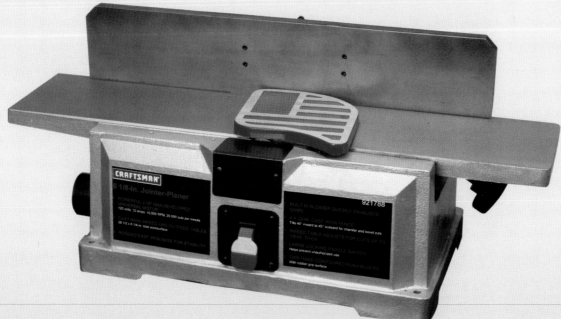

Types

Guess what. There are lots of types of jointers to choose from! Shocking, I know. Let's start small and work our way up.

Benchtop jointers exist and will provide some of the services you'll need. In general they're not my first recommendation. Benchtop or portable jointers are, by their nature, lighter than other models. They have shorter bed lengths (30" [762mm] as an average) and are most commonly powered by a universal motor in the 10-amp range. They are also usually outfitted with two knives in the cutterhead. So what's wrong with this? Let's start with the shorter beds. When working to straighten a board, it's generally important to have about three-quarters of the length of the board supported on the table in the middle of the cut. With the shorter bed length, you're limited in the length of board you can accurately joint. Now, you can make them work, and in many cases they'll be alright for jointing lumber up to about 48" (1219mm) in length. But should you be comfortable handicapping yourself from the start? It's possible your woodworking may not suffer from the shorter beds. And price is a significant consideration as well. Benchtop jointers run about $200 to $250. If most of your work is of smaller scale, the bed length may be just perfect.

Next: the knives. Two knives will produce a less clean than three or four knives will cut. "Clean" is determined by the number of knife marks that will be visible on the jointed surface. Because a board is run over the cutterhead at an average speed, the rotation of the knives produces a jointer-measuring statistic called cuts per minute (cpm). The more cuts per minute, the tighter together the knife marks occur and the less obvious they are. So, if you have a jointer with two knives and a jointer with four knives both running the same speed, the four-knife jointer will have twice as many cuts per inch

and leave a cleaner surface.

The motor size will determine the depth of cut that is possible in one pass. With a smaller motor, lighter cuts are required. This isn't a huge problem, because most surfacing passes shouldn't be deeper than a $^1/_{16}$" (2mm) in one pass anyway (and $^1/_{32}$" [0.8mm] is a better idea in woods with complicated grain patterns). But it will cause you to slow down a little for more dense woods.

Another limiting factor in most benchtop jointers is the possible width of cut. These machines are available in mostly 4"-wide (102mm) capacities and some 6"-wide (152mm) cut configurations. If most of your work is on smaller-scale lumber, the 4" (102mm) model may be adequate. But when you're working to maintain the beauty of the wood in your project, the wider the board the better. And a tabletop made up of 4"-wide (102mm) strips isn't pretty. So if you're buying a benchtop, go for the 6" (152mm).

When you move up to a traditional floor model 6" (152mm) jointer, you're guaranteed a 6"-wide (152mm) cut (some models will actually take a $6^1/_8$"-wide [155mm] pass), longer tables, an extra knife (we're up to three now), a more powerful induction motor (1 to $1^1/_2$ hp) and a floor-situated machine. As with some table saws, there are manufacturers who are producing benchtop models sitting on a stand of some sort that can be confusing. If it's sitting on a stand, don't automatically assume it's a three-knife, induction-powered machine. These 6" (152mm) jointers traditionally have tables averaging about 46" (1168mm) in length. Some manufacturers are now offering 6" (152mm) jointers with tables equal to the length found on 8" (203mm) jointers (about 66" [1676mm]), but there is a price increase.

Another change in the floor model is the introduction of a rabbeting ledge. Most benchtop machines will not offer this feature. Okay, now for some hon-

esty. I've never used a jointer to cut a rabbet on a board. That's what routers are for. However, if you need to make a very wide rabbet, a router won't be able to accomplish that task, whereas a jointer can, but so can a table saw. So I honestly wouldn't use this feature as a shopping criterion, but I had to tell you.

Overall, a 6" (152mm) jointer is a good choice for 60 percent of the woodworking world. It's got adequate capacity (both width and length) and adequate power. Expect to pay anywhere from $350 to $600 for the average 6" (152mm) jointer. That longer-bed jointer will run about $750.

The next step (and the highest we'll go here) is an 8" (203mm) jointer. With an 8" (203mm) jointer, the cut width increases to... you guessed it, 8" (203mm). You will also see longer beds (66" [1676mm] to 77" [1956mm] long), you'll often gain another knife and the motor will be more powerful to handle the increased width capacity. Motors will range from $1^1/_2$ hp 110-volt induction motors on up to 3 hp 220-volt motors.

These are the jointers that every woodworker should aspire to. Though a 6" (152mm) jointer is good and very useful, if you're serious about your woodworking, having the ability to surface an 8" (203mm) board is key. Most lumber isn't likely to be available in 10" (254mm) or 12" (305mm) widths, but you will frequently stumble across boards that are up to 8" (203mm) wide, and these should be highly prized. Finding a beautiful $7^3/_4$" (197mm) board and then having to rip it to less than 6" (152mm) so you can run it through your jointer is sad. Shoot for an 8" (203mm) for those times when you need it, and beyond that, the performance (even for surfacing a 5" [127mm] board) is worth the money. Speaking of money, expect to pay between $650 and $1,900 for an 8" (203mm) jointer, with the average price coming in around $1,000.

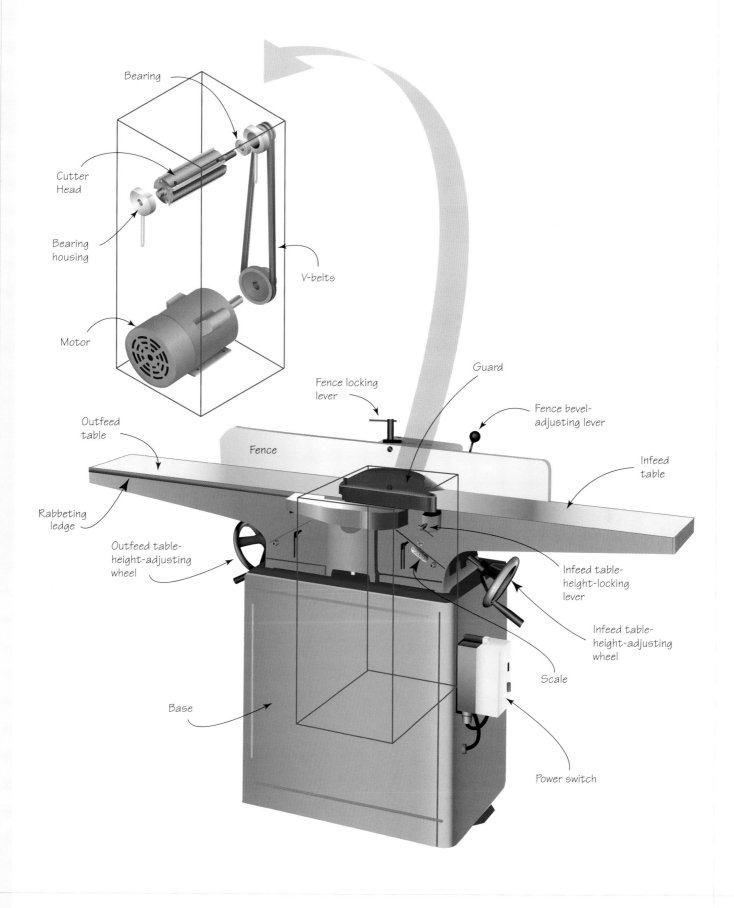

Bearing

Cutter
Head

Bearing
housing

Motor

V-belts

Outfeed
table

Fence

Fence locking
lever

Guard

Fence bevel-
adjusting lever

Infeed
table

Rabbeting
ledge

Outfeed table-
height-adjusting
wheel

Infeed table-
height-locking
lever

Infeed table-
height-adjusting
wheel

Scale

Base

Power switch

The Parts

One variable you will encounter in all the jointer categories is how the infeed table height is adjusted. Choosing between the two most common options (hand wheels or a lever) is mostly a personal preference. Neither is "better" than the other. Levers have the advantage of more rapidly adjusting the height with a single motion. Hand wheels have the advantage of more evenly and measurably adjusting the height (one-half revolution equaling $1/128$" [0.2mm], or something like that). Again, this is going to be a personal preference. I'd suggest getting the opportunity to try each to see which feels most comfortable to you.

You can tell how much the infeed table is moved by using the scale. Most scales are reasonably imprecise, with poor markings. You want to use them mostly as a guide to get you in the ballpark. Happily, you don't usually set a jointer by incremental changes. It's more a feel thing. So the scale is nice, but don't count on it.

Another important part of the jointer is a fence that runs across both tables and the cutterhead. This fence is a handy guide when a board is run with the wide face flat against the tables, but it is most important when the jointer is used to straighten an edge of a board. Then the fence is used to keep the board at a right angle to the tables, producing a square edge.

Listen closely. There's another part of a jointer that needs to stay in place — the guard. This spring-loaded piece of metal covers the cutterhead at all times and moves out of the way as the board is pushed across the knives. In fact the guard moves only enough to allow just the board through. There's only one reason to remove the guard and that's for making rabbet cuts. The jointer can appear deceptively safe. The knives are spinning in a small gap, and nothing is sticking up above the table as on a table saw. But don't be fooled. I don't want to get gory here, but if you

get cut on a table saw, they may be able to reattach what gets cut. On a jointer, there's nothing to reattach. So leave the guard in place, please.

Jointers can be used for other operations besides flattening and squaring boards. Many can be used to cut rabbets (two-sided trenches cut along the edge of a board). This is the operation that will require you to remove

the guard, but please put it back after you've made your rabbet. You can also do tapering operations on a jointer (such as for table legs), and you can use a jointer to cut chamfers and even shape round tenons on the ends of boards. Bottom line, whether you're just prepping a board or doing joinery on your jointer, this is a machine you want in your shop.

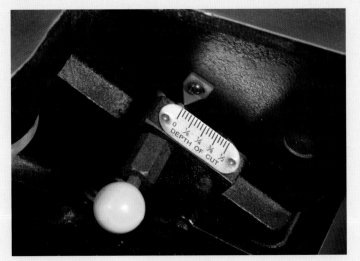

The height scale shown here has a decent scale and a pointer that will tell you where you are. It also offers another nice feature with the big knob. This is actually a lock that will keep you from accidentally moving the infeed table height. Not a necessity, but it is handy.

There is a little over 1" (25mm) spacing left between these belts when "pinched." This will work, but I prefer a tighter belt. The belt can be awkward to adjust. You'll need to loosen the motor mount bolts and slide the motor away from the cutterhead, while keeping the two pulley faces in parallel. If you've got a buddy, this is a good time to give him a call. Checking belt tension is an "every-now-and-then" procedure.

Maintenance

Jointers are actually fairly maintenance free, which is great because woodworking is about building things, not maintaining tools. A couple of things should be checked at setup and a few more that should be done routinely. The hardest part is maintaining the knives, and I'll give you some opinions on that shortly.

When you first set up your new jointer, you should, of course, read the instructions. They might help some. Then read this. If you're lucky, the machine arrives mostly assembled. You may need to attach the guard and the fence, but likely the motor will be attached. If not, do read the instructions. Even if the motor is attached already, your first maintenance activity should be to align the pulleys between the motor and the cutterhead. This is done using a straightedge or ruler. You want the rims of the two pulleys to be parallel with one another. This will keep your jointer running with fewer vibrations.

Another part of setup and maintenance relating to the belts is the tension on the belts. If you can pinch the belt sides together and make them touch, you have way too much slack on those belts. A good rule of thumb is that the belts should be at least 1" (25mm) apart after applying reasonable tension. Personally, I like my belts tighter than that. The tighter the better and less chance of slipping during operation.

Right out of the crate or box, you'll also need to clean off some goop from the metal surfaces. This is Cosmoline or some variation of it. It's a petroleum-based jelly that's been protecting metal from rust for a very long time. Use a little naptha and a bunch of paper towels to get the surface clean. Watch the knives when you're cleaning around the mouth opening. They're still sharp even when they're not running.

The beds, or tables of a jointer, are pretty important. Before we even look at making sure they're set up right, let's talk about taking care of their surface.

Yuck! What kind of a lame wood-worker would let a machine look like this!? Well, one that works in a garage in the Midwest. It doesn't take long for surface rust to build up. Granted, this should have been tackled a few months earlier.

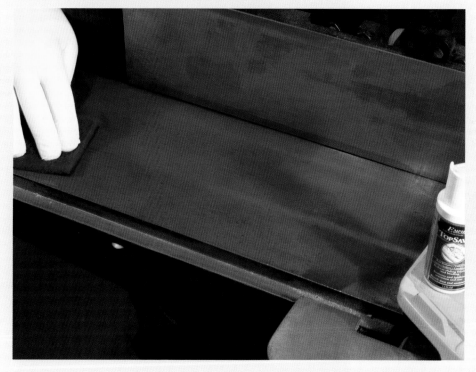

When you're using a rust remover, gloves are a good idea, and count on a little elbow grease. Don't miss the corners!

My jointer was sitting in a garage all winter without a whole lot of woodworking going on. When I pulled it out I was horrified to see the rust that had built up on the tables. But, because I'm an experienced tool guy, I knew it wasn't a crisis. Unless you're really a slacker and let it go for years, most rust that you'll find on the metal surface of a tool is surface rust. There are a number of products that you can use to take rust off of a tool. All work reasonably well, and some are more kind to your hands than others. I still recommend gloves, and you're still going to have to put some effort into the process.

The product I chose is Top Saver from Empire Manufacturing. It's a liquid slightly thicker than water, and you simply squirt or spray it onto the rusted surface. You can let it sit for a minute or so, but then it's time to get out the synthetic scrubbing pad.

That's a pretty impressive change. One more coat and it'll be ready to run.

A good straightedge is very useful for checking the tables of all your stationary tools. An adequate straightedge is also acceptable if you check it for straight and it doesn't flex while you're using it. Check each table front and back, then again diagonally (as shown) in a couple of places.

After checking the individual tables, you need to check the infeed and outfeed tables against each other. Again, measure both at the front and rear of the tables.

Once you scrub the surface for a while (it looks like an awful mess), it's time to wipe the surface clean with a clean cloth. That's when your short work suddenly comes to fruition. Honestly, this surface was achieved with no more than five minutes of work. It's not done. You can still see some embedded rust on the fence. So another application is required, with a final top coat to further protect the steel. But all in all, this is a pretty impressive transformation.

Okay, now that the tables and fence are all pretty, let's get to setting things right. To get a true cut on a jointer the infeed and outfeed tables need to be flat and parallel with one another. If the infeed table is canted a $1/2°$ to the left compared to the outfeed tables, you'll be making parallelograms with your wood. First, check the flatness of the individual tables using a reliable straightedge. Check along the length of the table both at the front and back of the table's width. Then lay your straightedge corner-to-corner on the table as well. A $1/64$" (0.4mm) gap isn't perfect, but it is acceptable. If you've got a significant gap anywhere on the table ($1/16$" [2mm]), you may want to consider returning the machine. If that gap happens at one of the outer corners of the table, it's not as major a concern.

Next, run the infeed table up to the same height as the outfeed table, and place your straightedge across both tables, again both at the front and back of the tables' width. The tables should be in line (parallel) with each other. If you find that the tables are even at one side or the other but not across the width, check your manual for opportunities to correct this. It's possible to shim the ways (the grooves that the beds move in) to correct this offset, but it's not an easy task. It's unusual for jointers to leave a factory out of parallel across the width of the beds. But if it happens and you can't or don't want to fix it, you've got a good argument for demanding a replacement.

Gotta add a comment here. All

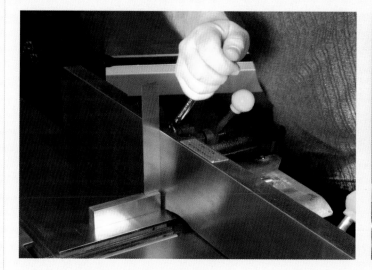

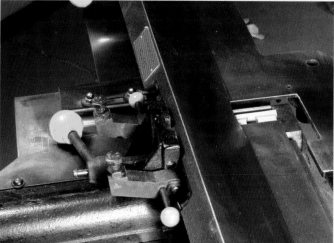

While checking the fence squareness with your engineer's square, you'll need to adjust the 90° stop. Often this stop consists of a bolt with a jamb nut. This is a simple design, but it really doesn't need to be much more complicated. Sneak up on the adjustment, then lock it in place.

There are a number of good reasons to use a jointer with the fence set at a 45° bevel... if it's set correctly. Otherwise, just don't bother.

jointer instruction manuals will tell you not to move or lift the jointer by the tables. Doing this could move the tables (bending isn't really likely... at least you hope not) and move them out of parallel. If you've ever moved a jointer you've probably noticed that there isn't really any other good place to grab the jointer except for the tables. I've been moving jointers for 20 years and I've yet to throw one out of whack by lifting at the tables. That doesn't mean you should jerk the entire weight at one end — take it slow and lift carefully and you'll be fine.

After determining that the tables are in good shape, it's time to check the fence. You should check the length of the fence for flatness, just as you did with the tables. You're much more likely to get a bow in the fence because the iron is thinner. I wish I could tell you that most jointer fences are perfect, but slight deviations are actually more the norm. If your fence is out less than 1/16" (2mm) along the full length, accept it. The truth is, if you try to return the fence to get a perfect one, you may end up with one that's worse.

Can you fix the fence yourself? Well, that reminds me of a story. A number

This 6" (152mm) jointer offers a separate stop for the 45° angle. With the 90° stop in place, the fence is accurately stopped at 90°.

By kicking the 90° stop out of the way, the 45° stops are now inline and ready to work.

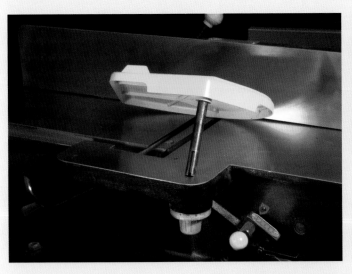

Most jointer guards are attached to a rod that slips into a space in the tables.

As the guard is lowered into place, a spring-loaded mechanism is held in tension until the guard rod is in place. This may take a couple of tries, but keep at it until the tension is correct.

of years back I was testing a jointer and found a fence that was out about ¹/₈" (3mm) across the length. When I contacted the manufacturer (who was and continues to be reputable), I was told it would be easier for me to fix it myself. I was told to remove the fence and put two 2×4 blocks on the floor, then lay the fence across the boards, bow up. Then, I should stand on the center of the fence. Honest, that's what I was told. Guess what — it worked.

You should always check the tables and fence for flatness when the tool is new. It is possible that the tables can come out of parallel (lifting by the tables maybe?), and if you're noticing difficulties in flattening a board, you may want to check this. It's much more likely that the fence can move out of square to the tables. That's why this check should be part of your routine maintenance. In fact, I've seen a situation where the spring on the guard was strong enough that each time it dropped back into place against the fence, it knocked the fence slightly out of square. Checking the fence is something that should be considered routine maintenance. Before each new project, take a second to check the fence for square and adjust as necessary. It's much easier than rerunning all your lumber.

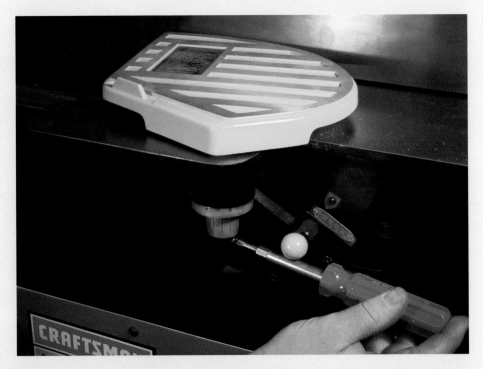

Most guard spring mechanisms will have some type of locking mechanism to keep the guard from working loose. Don't skip this step.

So, after you've checked your fence for flat, you need to check it for square to the tables. Jointer fences are designed to bevel, always in one direction (to the rear), but sometimes in both directions. The fence mechanism usually includes some type of detent setting for returning the fence to a 90° angle to the tables. This is what we want to check. By placing your reliable engineer's square

against the fence and table you can confirm the 90° setting of the mechanism. Check at both ends of the fence in case there's a twist in the fence. If there's a significant twist, get out the 2×4s.

While you're checking for 90°, you should also check for 45°, because most jointers offer a stop at this setting. Use the same procedures, then set it and forget it until your next maintenance period.

If your guard is slamming home after each pass, you can adjust the tension on the guard. This also applies after removing the guard for rabetting. Each jointer's mechanism is slightly different, but your manual should have instructions on adjusting this tension. Just make sure the guard continues to completely cover the knives after each pass.

Knives

For a jointer to work correctly, the knives need to be set at the exact depth in the cutter so that they are even at the tip with the height of the outfeed table. What does that mean? It means that, unlike the knives in a planer, the depth setting of the knives in relation to the cutterhead is not the critical setting. Because of this, knife-setting jigs are different for jointers and planers. You can use a setting jig for jointers, but they're still problematic. I still opt for good old eyesight and a trusty rule.

To check the knives for proper depth, set your straightedge on the outfeed table and extend it over the cutterhead (with the machine unplugged and the guard temporarily held away from the fence). Carefully rotate the cutterhead (I strongly recommend gloves here) until the lead edge of one of the knives is at the top of its rotation and touching the straightedge. Repeat this check on each of the knives to make sure they're all set correctly.

Now let's look at what to do if the machine is delivered with the knives improperly set (not usually the case), or if your knives are dull and need to be sharpened: removing, replacing and resetting the knives.

There's actually another reason to do this. Jointer knives can be nicked in one spot. This can happen if a staple, nail or even mineral deposit is left in the wood prior to jointing. In fact, even knots in the wood can nick a knife. When this happens, a raised line will appear on the surface of the wood, along the length of the board. This will

happen to all jointers. One way to reduce this occurrence is to replace the standard high-speed steel knives with carbide knives. The harder carbide will hold up to general abuse and provide about double the life between sharpenings. It will also increase the cost quite a bit, so you need to determine if it's worth the expense to you.

You might have heard another woodworker say that carbide knives can't be sharpened to as fine an edge as high-speed steel knives. Carbide manufacturing has improved significantly over the past few years and carbide will take a very good edge. That said, no matter how sharp your high-speed steel knives are, after the first 20 board feet of lumber that keen edge will be dulled and you'd be hard pressed to notice a difference between carbide and high-speed steel — except that you'll get twice the life out of the carbide edge.

Okay, wow, I wandered off topic there. Back to the nicks. Knives don't always have to be replaced or sharpened if nicks appear. In most jointers there is a slight amount of left-to-right play in the knives' fit in the cutterhead. By offsetting the knives slightly to the left or right you may be able to get an undamaged section of the other knife (or knives) to cut where the nick is and remove the marks. Now, usually the knives can be offset only by about $1/16$" (2mm) or $1/8$" (3mm) at the most, so you won't always be able to overcome the nick, but it's worth a try. So, let's go back to removing the knives.

There are slight differences in each jointer as to how the knives are held in place, but in general a steel bar with tightening bolts is adjusted against the knife to hold it in place in a channel in the cutterhead. The number of bolts will vary according to the width of the cutterhead. The height of the knives is controlled by either springs, set screws or both. To remove the knife, the guard is moved to the side (and the machine unplugged). Rather than remove the guard and have to reset the tension, a

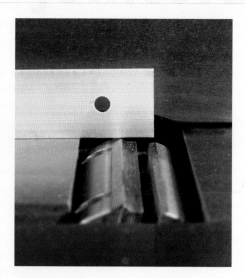

Your jointer will not work properly if the knives aren't adjusted even in height to the outfeed table height. The tricky part here is determining when the knife (each of the three knives, not just one!) reaches the top of its rotation. Jointers don't have head locks to lock the cutterhead in place, making this task more difficult. The quick rule of thumb is to adjust only one knife at a time, using the other knives as a height reference.

squeeze clamp can be attached to the guard to hold it in the open position.

Jointers don't traditionally have a cutterhead lock (a mechanism that will keep the head from turning), but the tension of the belt and motor should provide adequate holding power. Start loosening the bolts from either end of the knife, leaving the center bolt until last. You don't have to do more than loosen the bolts a few turns. You save the center bolt till last because there's a very good chance that the knives have a set of springs behind them. When you release the last bolt the knife isn't going to jump out of the machine, but if your hands are in the wrong place and you're not prepared, you can definitely cut yourself. With all the bolts loosened, the knife should pop free. Carefully lift the knife out of the slot. If you've got a small magnet, using it to pull the knife free is safer than grabbing it with your fingers. If the knife doesn't lift free easily, you may need a couple more turns on some of the bolts.

Loosening the gib plate requires working close to the sharp knives. And, because the head is likely to move, it's best to use a glove on your other hand and hold the cutterhead still while you loosen the bolts. Beware of slipping while loosening the bolts.

With the blade removed you can see down into the gullet and check for springs. If they get away from you, they're heck to find.

With the gib plate removed, as well as the blade, you can easily see into the gullet. Now's a good time to clean. Don't bump the set screw if you can avoid it.

Once the knife is free, you should be able to see into the slot and see the set screws. If you're still having a hard time seeing, remove the knife gib (the clamping block). The set screws should be easy to see now.

If you're just offsetting the knives to correct a nick, you don't have to do a thing to the set screws. In fact, it would be bad if you did. But while you've got things open, a few seconds to clean out any dust is time well spent. Again, in just adjusting the knives you should pay attention to the knife orientation in the cutterhead before loosening the last bolt. This will help you determine which way to shift the knife. After shifting the knife, you can simply apply even pressure along the length of the knife (wear gloves, or use a rag to avoid the sharp edge) till you can feel it press against the set screws. Then, tighten the center bolt. I usually follow the center bolt with the two outside bolts, making sure the knife stays seated against the set screws, then tighten the remaining bolts.

If you've sharpened the knives or are putting in a new set of knives, you'll need to check the knife height against the outfeed table height. Replace only one knife at a time, using the height setting of one of the previously set knives to help you set the first replacement knife. Then use that knife as a guide to set the other knives. You'll need to adjust the set screws to match the height of the reset knives, then use the set screws to fine-tune the setting. It's my opinion that springs just get in the way in this process. You can easily remove them while adjusting the set screws, then replace them before tightening the gib in place.

One comment on a new development in jointers: spiral or helical cutterheads. Traditionally, the knives in jointers are high-speed, single-edged steel knives that can be sharpened when they become dull. They are set in the cutterhead so they are perpendicular to the fence and leave evenly

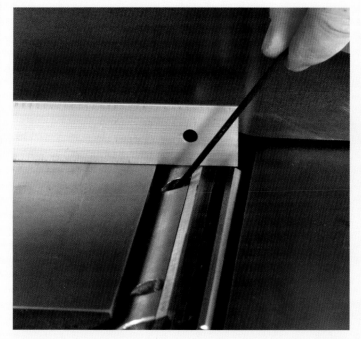

The set screws will usually require a hex or Allen wrench to adjust. A slight turn of the screw can make a dramatic change, so don't work too quickly. If the springs were in place on this jointer, there would be no way I could set the knife height without holding the blades in place.

These small carbide inserts are deceptively powerful. They've made me a happy jointer user by removing the need for careful knife setup, as well as more than quadrupling the time required between knife changes. Get them if you can afford it. Enough said.

spaced, small lines or jointer marks across the board. These lines aren't a concern because your board's next stop is the planer and the marks will disappear. But a design that's creeping into consumer machinery from the industrial world is the spiral cutterhead. This variation is either a set of small ($1/8"$ × $1/2"$ × $1/2"$ [3mm × 13mm × 13mm]) carbide cutters (inserts), or disposable, flexible high-speed steel knives twisted into position on the cutterhead in a spiral pattern much like the pattern on a barber pole or candy cane. The cutters can be oriented with the cutting edge either skewed to match the spiral pattern or perpendicular to the fence as in a traditional knife.

The benefit in this design is twofold. The staggered or spiral orientation means that the cut is more of a skew than a straight slice. This produces a quieter cut and can provide a cleaner cut in some woods. The other benefit, which is most important to me, is that each of these carbide cutter inserts is four-sided, each with a fresh, sharp

edge. Even better, the insert fits into the head only one way, so you don't have to worry about setting the knife height. When you get a nick or the edge starts to dull, you only need to release the hold-down screw and rotate the insert one-quarter turn, then tighten it down again. Wonderful!

Now, you're right — not only are these cutterheads more expensive but the knives can be more expensive than standard knives. But the cost is quickly balanced by the convenience of the knives, and in the case of the four-edged carbide inserts, great longevity.

Other Maintenance

Routine maintenance on a jointer is pretty simple. You need to keep the tables and fence face free from rust and add your choice of lubricant occasionally. Depending on the size and com-

A less expensive alternative to the carbide inserts is this disposable spiral knife system. About two-thirds the cost of the insert head, the disposable knives run around $15 a set and are just as easy to install. It's a good option that actually provides a slightly better finished cut.

plexity of the machine, you may need to oil one or two moving areas. Check your manual to determine this need and the oiling locations.

As mentioned, you should check the fence for square before each project, but other than that, your jointer will provide you with reliable, always-ready performance with just these simple steps. And don't forget to use your jointer with your planer; otherwise, the job is only half done!

planers

PLANERS ARE ONE OF THE really cool woodworking machines. They hog off material to make a board whatever thickness you want and give you two parallel faces on the board at the same time. Plus, they make a lot of cool shavings.

If you have a planer, you should have a jointer. These two tools need to work together to create flat, straight and square boards that are just the right size. Strangely enough, with the advent of portable, or benchtop, planers, many woodworkers are quick to buy these reasonably inexpensive machines first, and they hold off buying the more expensive jointer. Unfortunately, these machines should be bought in just the opposite order. A board should be run over the jointer before it goes to the planer.

Planers are one of just a couple of machines that have dramatically reduced the effort involved in woodworking. Along with the jointer, planers have simplified preparing a board. What was once a laborious task that took woodworkers hours with hand planes is now a half-hour of effortless motion.

Effortless, but it's also really boring. But don't get caught not paying attention when using the planer. Although you're just shoving boards in, it's important to pay attention to the way the boards are fed into the planer.

Each board has a grain direction. It's sort of like petting a cat. If you pet the board lengthwise with the grain, in both directions, you'll find that your hand will recognize the more smooth direction. This is the direction you want to run the board — with the grain.

Also, you need to flip the board repeatedly during planing. This flattens both surfaces and, more important, keeps the fresh wood evenly exposed on both sides. The wood is still a little wet inside and if you plane from only one face you can cause the board to warp by allowing the moisture to evaporate unevenly.

The Parts

There are only a few noteworthy parts to a planer: the table surface, usually made up of infeed and outfeed tables, with the center bed between; the motor that powers the cutterhead (equipped with two or three knives); and a mechanism to raise and lower either the cutterhead or the tables.

Another part is the rollers. A powered roller is positioned on the infeed side of the cutterhead to pull the wood toward the cutterhead. A non-powered roller positioned after the cutterhead is the pressure roller. Its only job is to keep the wood flat against the tables.

How It Works

After a board has been straightened and surfaced on one face using a jointer, it's ready for the planer. The planer will pass the board through the feed roller and past the cutterhead, removing an even amount of wood from the nonsurfaced face (the previously surfaced face is run against the tables). Because the wood is referenced off the table, the finished board will be as flat and straight as the first surfaced face and will also be parallel to that face. And that's hard to do with a hand plane.

Types

There are two distinct classes of planers: benchtop and stationary. Benchtop planers are designed to be lighter weight and portability (though I wouldn't want to carry one around for very long). This feature has actually become more advantageous for today's woodworker as a storage issue (sliding the planer into a cabinet when not in use) rather than taking the machine to the job site. Today's smaller shops benefit from the ability to store this occasionally used machine.

Portable planers are most commonly divided by the possible width of cut, ranging from 12" (305mm) to 13" (330mm). These planers use universal motors and are most commonly

equipped with two high-speed steel knives. Even with the universal motor these machines are capable of removing up to $1/8$" (3mm) of material in a single pass, though, don't expect to take that wide a cut on a 12"-wide (305mm) board. That's asking more of the machine than is reasonable.

The portable planer is not that old an invention and during the past 15 years the portable planer has become a much better machine, often rivaling stationary planers for features. Portable planers offer quick-change disposable knives, requiring no time to set the knives (one of my favorite features). The cost related to buying replacement knives is about the same as the cost of having the knives sharpened, so the benefits are pretty nice.

Also, portable planers are now beginning to offer feed speeds. This is a feature that had previously been found only on stationary machines. The benefit to this feature is the ability to improve the quality of the cut by slowing down the feed rate on the last pass, getting more cuts per inch.

Another more common feature on these machines is a head lock. One of the idiosyncrasies of planers is something called snipe. This shallow groove that occurs across the width of the board, usually about 1" (25mm) from the ends of the board (both at the infeed and outfeed end of the board) is caused by the cutterhead momentarily cutting too deeply into the board. This action is caused by a variety of things including the feed roller or pressure roller allowing the board to lift during the cut. The angle of the tables can also cause this. The head lock helps to hold the cutterhead in place, reducing the incidence of snipe.

Yes, I said reduce. Even the best

planers will produce some amount of snipe. Nearly perfect is about as good as you're going to find. But don't freak about this. Snipe is often about one- or two-thousandths of an inch deep and easily removed with sanding. So before you tear your machine apart to fix this imperfection, decide how bad the situation is. Most woodworkers have come to terms with this annoyance and simply leave a couple of extra inches in length on the board, then cut off the snipe. You need to square the ends of the board anyway, so this usually isn't a huge inconvenience.

Portable planers do a good job of surfacing a board. Priced between $200 and $500, even the most basic planer will do a decent job. The trade-off on the low price is that these machines aren't designed to run a couple thousand board feet of hard maple a week. If you're running a significant amount of lumber on a routine basis, you should step up to a stationary machine.

Stationary machines differ in construction materials and motor. These serious woodworking machines use induction motors that are up to the task of surfacing lots of lumber often. These machines are also constructed of cast iron and steel, whereas many of the parts on portable planers are aluminum and plastic. The tables are

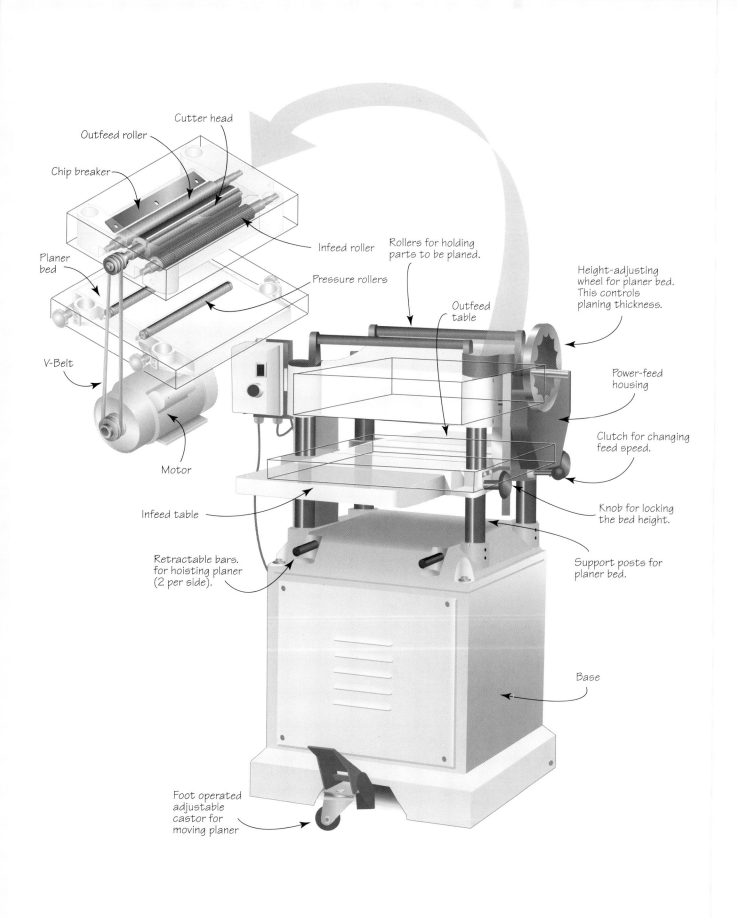

Cutter head

Outfeed roller

Chip breaker

Planer bed

V-Belt

Motor

Infeed roller

Infeed table

Pressure rollers

Rollers for holding parts to be planed.

Outfeed table

Height-adjusting wheel for planer bed. This controls planing thickness.

Power-feed housing

Clutch for changing feed speed.

Knob for locking the bed height.

Support posts for planer bed.

Retractable bars. for hoisting planer (2 per side).

Base

Foot operated adjustable castor for moving planer

more commonly steel, larger than on portable planers and beefy.

One thing that is available on stationary planers but not on portables is an adjustable table rather than an adjustable head. All that needs to happen in a planer is that the spinning knives and table need to come closer together. On portable planers the cutterhead and knives are moved closer to the table. On stationary planers some will move the cutterhead and others will move the table. In testing a number of models I've never seen a significant difference in cut quality between the two designs. But I prefer the design that moves the table because it allows the motor to be mounted below the table in the cabinet. This keeps the top of the machine obstruction-free (good for handing boards across) and also makes it much easier to get to the knives.

One addition on many stationary machines is a set of bed rollers. Just as they sound, these rollers are set slightly above the height of the machine's tables and help the wood pass the cutterhead. This is more important on these large machines because of the larger capacities. For home shop use, 12"-wide (305mm) and 15"-wide (381mm) planers are not uncommon and a 20" (508mm) planer is not out of the question. Because of this capacity, much larger lumber can be surfaced, and these boards are heavy. Just the friction of these boards dragging across the tables can affect the machine's performance, so adding the bed rollers can help significantly.

One of the specialty features on benchtop planers that is pretty much a standard on 15" (381mm) planers is the two-feed-speed option. Again, this will improve the cut on the final pass, and yes, these models also offer head locks. But rather than a bar that locks quickly, the larger planers need more control and use threaded knobs to lock the head (or table) in place for that final pass.

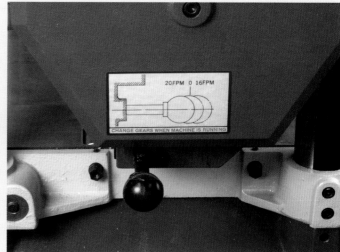

Bed rollers vary in design from machine to machine. There are usually two and they're usually steel, which is good. If you want to support a board, using a material that gives isn't very smart. Bed rollers are usually set to an accurate height in the factory, but they can get knocked out of alignment. If necessary, they can be adjusted. Again, each set of rollers is unique to each machine, so check your manual for instructions on adjusting the bed rollers.

The feed speed control on a 15" (381mm) planer is usually a simple lever. You may think you're supposed to move it left-to-right, but most actually operate by pushing in or pulling out. One thing, all the speed controls should be changed only while the machine is running. If you do it with the machine stopped you run the risk of damaging the gears.

When you add all this weight, you add a base or cabinet and it becomes a stationary machine. Another change is the increase to three knives, which provides a better quality of cut. Most knives in stationary planers are sharpenable high-speed steel. Carbide knives are available as upgrades, and some planers are now offering helical or spiral knives. This is a pricey upgrade, but it does provide quieter operation, and a smoother cut. It also offers easier knife setting and changing. It's not a common option yet, but keep your eyes open.

One constant in any planer model is the need for dust collection. No other machine in the shop removes as much material as a planer. As a kid I worked in a production woodworking shop with my dad. One of my first tasks was to be a "catcher" on a 20" (508mm) planer. I stood on the outfeed side of the machine and returned the boards to the guy on the "smart" side of the planer. That's all well and good, but at the time we didn't have the machine hooked up to dust collection. Trust me, it doesn't take long to be standing in a

pile of wood shavings that reaches to your knees — not to mention the dust cloud blowing around your face. Dust collectors are required. Period.

A couple of new portable models have actually made this a part of the machine. By using the motor to power an internal fan, these machines pull the shavings away from the cutterhead and deposit them in a simple bag or garbage can. That's okay for a portable planer, but a stationary unit will overwhelm a small fan. Hook your machine to a separate dust collector with adequate pull (500 to 750 cfm).

Although all planers have labels that tell you to keep your hands out of the planer mouth, that's not likely to happen all that often. It can happen when a board becomes stuck (wedged) in the machine, or when a board is too thin at a spot and doesn't connect with the feed rollers. In either case, please stop the machine before you let your hands pass the mouth (on either side) of the machine. The more common chance of accident on planers is simply in handling the knives for sharpening or setting. You're working in tight spaces

with wrenches and bolts and more than one woodworker has loosened a bolt with too much pressure and barked a knuckle into a blade. This is a good place to wear work gloves. Even dull knives are sharp enough to ruin your day.

Maintenance

There are a couple of basic things to check to make sure your machine will produce quality work. These checks don't have to happen very often but certainly on setting up the machine and then maybe once a year afterward.

First, the infeed and outfeed tables need to be aligned with the center table. If the feed tables are cast iron (as on many stationary models) they should align flush on the top surface as close to perfect as possible. A steel rule or reliable straightedge of adequate length to span both the center table and the feed table being adjusted is required.

If your machine has rollers rather than solid tables, these can be a little trickier to set up because you can't flush-up mating surfaces. Essentially, you still want to get the rollers even on the top surface with the center table. I've got to tell you, I've set up a number of these and it's a bit like picking a lock. You need to use both a crescent wrench and an Allen wrench at the same time to finesse these guys into place. But it'll be worth it.

If you're working with a portable planer the tables are likely fold-down and the height where the tables meet is fixed. But you can adjust the far end of the tables for a flat length across the span.

Now, here's a little trick if you're having snipe problems. Cut a board of stable (and flat) 3/4" (19mm) plywood that is slightly less wide than the capacity of your planer and make it long enough to span the entire length of the tables. That's infeed, outfeed and center tables. Screw a 3/4" × 3/4" (19mm × 19mm) strip to the underside of what will be the infeed end of your board.

This strip will act as a hook to keep the auxiliary table (that's what we're making) in place. Lay this across the tables and adjust the depth of cut on your planer to compensate for the 3/4" (19mm) plywood. You've now got a perfectly flat set of tables that will reduce your snipe significantly.

A couple of other occasional maintenance activities involve grease and oil. These mostly apply to larger planers, but the grease won't hurt the benchtop models either. Check your manual, or check the machine itself for locations that indicate routine oiling is required. Again, your manual will give you an indication of how often this should be done. This is a guideline, so don't freak out if you don't oil as soon as the manual recommends. Greasing is another topic. Most manuals won't tell you where to grease, but your common sense will tell you that the columns on your planer see the majority of metal-to-metal contact. Give 'em some grease every now and then. And while you're at it, smear some grease on the lift screw. It's that threaded rod that

meshes with gears to move the table or head up and down. Now you're ready to move on.

Okay, now the hard part: changing and setting the knives. Let's start simple with the benchtop models. It's almost impossible to find a benchtop planer these days that still uses traditional 1/8"-thick (3mm) knives that can be sharpened. I think that's a good thing because the disposable blades are easier to replace and setup accurately. Some blades will be single-sided, others will be double-sided, but all will have some way of aligning the blades on the cutterhead so they're set perfectly and accurately with no fuss. The pictures on pages 47-49 will give you the steps that should be very similar on all benchtop planers.

If you're working with a larger planer, then you'll almost certainly have standard knives. These machines were initially designed for commercial use, so the benefit of sharpening and the added durability of a full-sized knife make sense. You may see disposable knives slipping into this category some

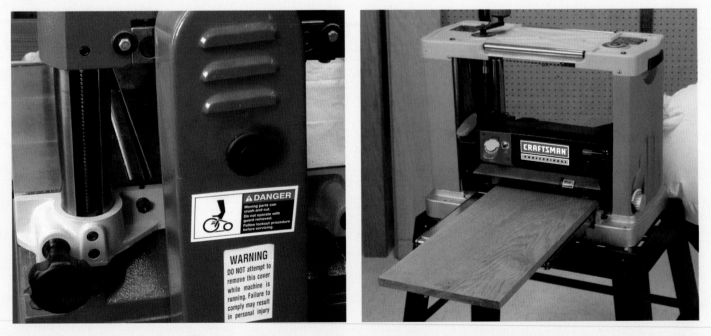

On this bottom-mounted motor planer, it's the tables that move. So the two head lock knobs (okay, I guess they're table lock knobs in this case) are mounted on the table itself and actually run threaded bolts up against the columns to lock the table.

This benchtop planer from Craftsman has a bag attached to the machine for collecting the chips pulled away from the cutterhead by the integral dust collection fan. Needless to say, you'll want to check that bag fairly often. If it gets overfull you'll have a real mess on your hands.

day, but we ain't there yet. Most of these full-sized machines will use gibs, set screws and often springs to lift the blades away from the cutterhead. They replace and set similar to the knives on a jointer, with one significant difference. The knives on a jointer are set to a height where they are even (at the top of the cutterhead swing) with the outfeed table. On a planer the knives have to be set only at the same height as the other knives. The movement of the head or table takes care of the relationship of the knives to the wood. That's why jigs are easier to use on a planer.

The photos on the following pages will walk you through the steps to set up the knives on a planer.

Last bit of maintenance advice: As with any of the major pieces of woodworking machinery that have cast-iron tables, keeping them clean and well lubricated (whether with paraffin or a spray) will keep them protected against rust and also help the wood move easier. This goes for steel tables on portable units as well. Keep the tool clean and well tuned and it'll take care of you for a long time.

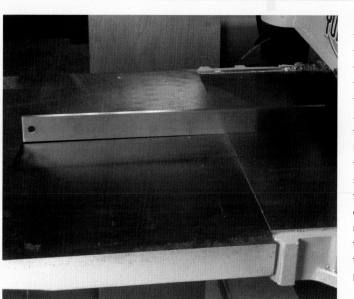

Frequently, cast-iron tables are machined to mate perfectly with the center table. Three or four machine bolts attach the feed tables, and there's little adjustment but flushing up the top surface. Should you find that the tables don't align flat, you may need to shim the joint between the tables to compensate.

I'll be honest: I'm not a big fan of infeed and outfeed roller tables. They're difficult to adjust, I'm always dropping stuff between the rollers and they don't provide very stable support. The one good thing is that because of the serious spring tension on the feed and pressure rollers on the larger machines, the feed tables are mostly just to keep you from dropping boards on the floor. The center table will support the board adequately to protect against most snipe.

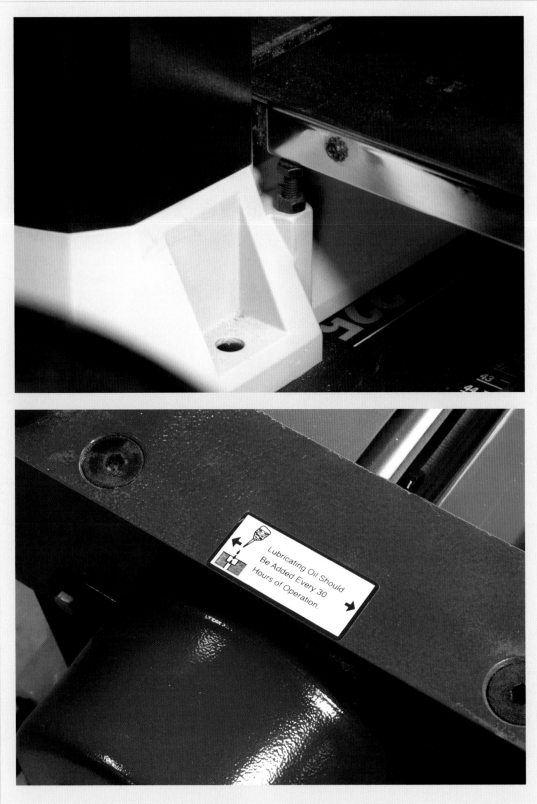

All the benchtop planers have a variation of a bolt with a jamb nut to adjust the infeed and outfeed tables height. Some will require crescent wrenches (as the one shown here), and others will use Allen wrenches. The best of the lot will allow you to adjust the tables while in the down position. The one shown here just makes the cut because the bolt is located close to the edge of the table.

Subtle, right? Get the message, read the instructions and feed your machine the fluids it needs when it needs them.

On benchtop planers, the cutterhead is always protected by some type of cover. You usually have to remove four or more bolts or screws to access the knives. Some of these bolts may also do double duty holding the chip deflector/collector attachment in place. Once the bolts are loose, the cover should lift free easily.

With the cover removed, the blade holder (a metal bar screwed across the blade) is visible. One nice feature is that when this cover is removed, a head lock automatically drops into place, allowing the head to move only enough to position the knives for removal. Good for safety and good for knife changing.

Now all you have to do is remove the 92 screws holding the blade holder in place. Okay, it's usually more like nine, but by the time you get them all out it seems like more. Fair warning here: Many of these screws are put in place by pneumatic tools and are often tighter than they should be. It may take some serious force to break the screws loose. I've also run into situations where the screw material was, how shall I put it? Crap. And rather than break the screw loose, the head was stripped. If this happens to you, remove the screw any way you can (cut a slot in the head and use a regular screwdriver) and buy a set of replacement screws made of a better quality steel.

With the holder removed, you can see the disposable blade nestled on its alignment pins (man, I love those). You can also see the spring that supports the holder. (It's not all that useful. If you lose one, don't sweat it.) And at the far left of the photo is the head lock release. You'll need to hold that down to rotate the head to the next blade position.

If you're not wearing gloves to handle the blade, then don't. In this case. Delta has included a magnetic tool that allows you to remove the blade without really having to touch it. You can use any magnet you have around the shop to do the same if one isn't included on your planer. Once you've reversed or replaced the blade over the alignment pins, put the holder back in place and insert the screws. Out of habit I still prefer to start with a center screw, then tighten the two end screws and finally fill in the screws in between.

Accessing the knives on a 15" (381mm) planer usually requires removing the dust deflector. You may need to remove a chip guard to more easily access the gib bolts, though. Note that I'm wearing a glove to hold the head. Larger planers don't have head locks (they should) so you end up having to steady the head as you loosen the bolts.

With the bolts sufficiently loosened you will be able to lift the blade free of the head. The gib (the metal clamping bar with the bolts in it) can remain in the cutterhead. However, if there's lots of dust in the head, you may want to lift out the gib and do a little cleaning while you're in there.

Almost universal in 15" (381mm) planers is the use of set screws and springs. The springs help lift the blades free of the head for replacement, but they can be annoying when resetting the knives. If the planer doesn't have set screws, the springs are very important, though.

Hopefully, you have a set of sharp knives handy or you're sharpening your own knives. If you have to wait for your knives to come back from being sharpened, you'll need to make sure you hang on to all the small parts from the head.

Whether your knives are replacements or freshly sharpened, the knife height will need to be reset. Most manufacturers will recommend a certain extension height above the cutterhead. It shouldn't be more than $\frac{1}{8}$" (3mm). A jig can be extremely helpful in setting the knives. Hopefully you won't run into the problem I did here. Though a very nice knife-setting jig, it was useless in this case because the head opening on this planer didn't allow both legs of the jig to grab (they're magnets) the cutterhead. Normally, it's a simple matter of dialing in the required knife projection on the center guide and allowing the jig to push the knife against the springs while you tighten the gib bolt. Start in the center of the knife, then do both ends. You won't need the jig to tighten the rest of the bolts.

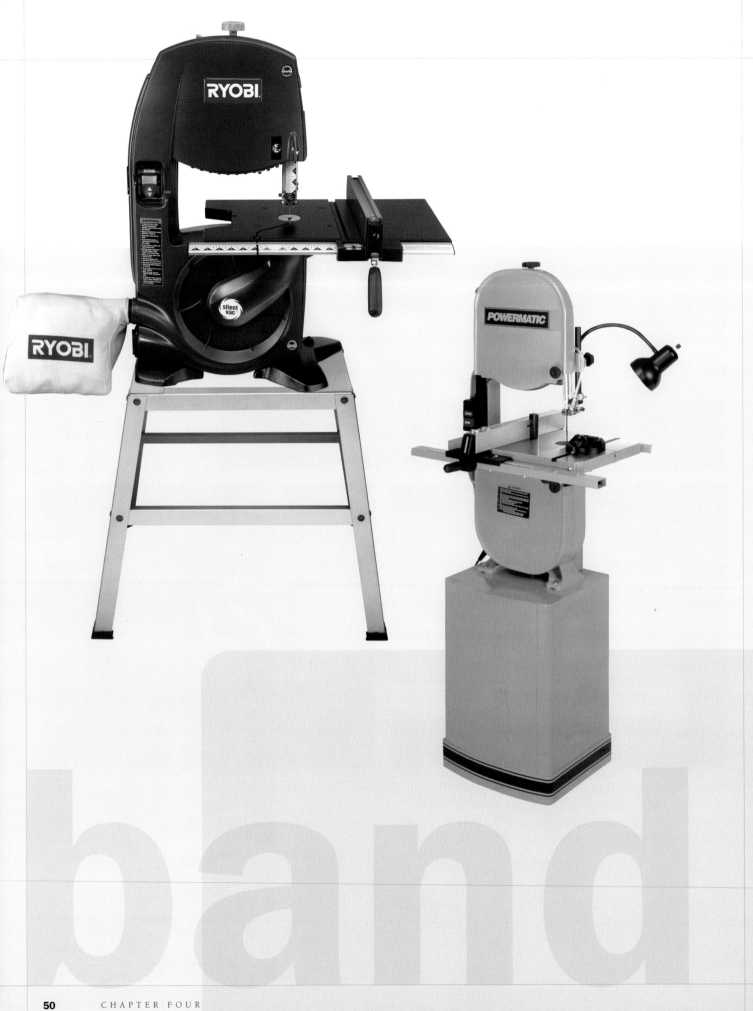

band saws

IN MANY EUROPEAN WORKSHOPS the band saw is the central piece of woodworking machinery, as the table saw is in the United States. This prominence is borne of space concerns because the band saw takes up a lot less space than a table saw, and space is even more of a premium in shops on the other side of the Atlantic.

Some of the European affection for the band saw may be connected to the fact that it's older technology than the table saw. The concept of pulling a straight blade with sharp teeth through wood predates the circular-shaped saw blade by millennia.

Two-handed pit saws were used as far back as Egyptian times and were definitely a strong part of tradition with the early Americans who explored and developed the interior of the North America.

The band saw is a close relative of those early saws. Although the idea of wrapping the straight blade into a continuous circle is a newer one, and adding a motor certainly is more recent, the action used by a band saw has been in use for a very long time. Happily, by making the blade a continuous loop and adding a motor we managed to make it a one-person job with a lot less backbreaking effort.

So there's nothing wrong with being fond of the band saw as a primary woodworking machine. When properly tuned and maintained a band saw is capable of accurate, straight cuts, but it can also resaw lumber and cut simple or complicated curves. It's a good universal machine, and though I won't call it the most important machine in my shop, I wouldn't want a shop without one.

Types

Band saws are available in various sizes and designs. In most cases they are a two-wheeled machine (one up, one down) with a table in between the wheels and a motor connected to the bottom wheel. The blade is a continuous circle tensioned against both the wheels, and the cutting takes place where the blade passes through the table. There are also three-wheeled versions that allow for a wider cut in material without significantly increasing the size of the machine. Some of these are excellent; others are simply difficult to keep aligned because of the additional third wheel.

Both benchtop and stationary models are available. The critical measurement on band saws (and the measurement used to define the categories) is the dimension from the inside of the column joining the upper and lower wheel housings and the blade itself. So a 14" (356mm) band saw will allow you to cut up to 14" (356mm) between the column and blade. That's an approximation, because often you get a little less than 14" (356mm), but that's the general concept.

Band saws run from 9" (229mm) cut capacity on up to 20" (508mm) and more, but the most common size is a 14" (356mm) saw. Prices can range from under $100 for a small benchtop to over $2,500 for a quality 17" (432mm) floor model. Motor size will also range widely, from small ⅓ hp universal motors up to 3 hp 220-volt induction motors. Although cut capacity is important, I think motor size is more so.

Parts

Because of the way a band saw works, the motor's power is transferred to a lot of moving parts to achieve a cut. It has to spin both the wheels at a pretty high speed, and the blade needs to be accurately aligned and tightened against the wheels to achieve a quality cut. If the motor is underpowered for the task (and this is especially important when resawing) the inertia necessary to make a successfully cut just isn't there. Yes, adjusting the type of blade for each operation is important (more on this later), but if your motor is too small, you can't overcome that very easily.

Another consideration is the design of the saw body. Traditionally, the band saw has been a two-piece cast-iron construction with upper and lower wheel housings bolted together at the column. No matter what anyone says, there's nothing wrong with this design for most band saw tasks — even resawing. In fact, this design allows you to increase the cutting height capacity by adding a riser block between the two housings, adding an extra 6" (152mm). That's very handy and an affordable ($60) upgrade. You'll need to buy longer blades, but it's worth the investment.

A design growing in popularity is a steel cabinet design from Europe. The steel upper and lower cabinets are attached to one another by a folded steel column that runs the entire height of the machine. This column provides strong, lightweight support for the machine while still providing good blade tension. Both are good designs and will provide quality service. While the cast-iron saw design allows for a riser block, the steel frame is fixed at this position and can't be expanded. Because of this, it's important to make sure the resaw capacity is adequate for your needs.

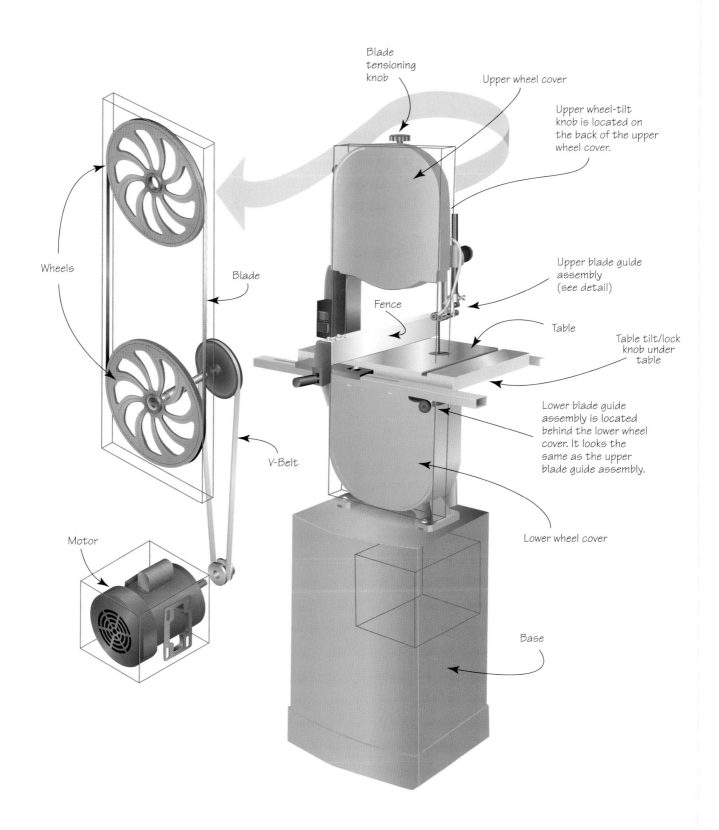

Blade tensioning knob

Upper wheel cover

Upper wheel-tilt knob is located on the back of the upper wheel cover.

Wheels

Blade

Fence

Upper blade guide assembly (see detail)

Table

Table tilt/lock knob under table

Lower blade guide assembly is located behind the lower wheel cover. It looks the same as the upper blade guide assembly.

V-Belt

Motor

Lower wheel cover

Base

Maintenance

When it comes to maintaining a band saw, there's a fair amount to know, even for basic maintenance. Because of the way the blade tracks in a circle riding on the two wheels, it takes only a little misalignment to affect the cut. Let's start from the top down.

Looking at the back of the upper wheel housing you will see two adjustment knobs. The top knob is the tensioning knob. By turning this knob you raise and lower the upper wheel, spreading the distance between the two wheels — that's how the blade is tensioned. Some saws are now equipped with a quick tensioning device that allows you to completely release the tension on the blade with the flick of a lever. It also allows you to tension the saw instantly to the proper tension (as long as you haven't changed the blade width). This is smart and convenient. Smart because it's generally accepted that it's harmful to the blade and wheel bearings to remain under tension. The quick-release lever makes it convenient to extend the life of your saw.

You'll be able to tell if your blade is tensioned correctly (at least by the book) by looking at the tensioning gauge at the back of the saw. It's marked for the multiple widths of blades that can be used on the saw. Large saws with more powerful motors will accept wider blades. All those things work together to make the saw more efficient at resawing larger pieces of wood.

The tension gauge isn't the bible. It's a good guide to get you in the ballpark. Different blade designs allow you to use the saw with less tension. And many woodworkers prefer to tension the blade past the recommended position on the saw for a more accurate cut. This is another one of those variables in woodworking machinery that you'll need to come to grips with for yourself through trial and error.

The other important knob on the back of the saw is the tracking knob. What it's really doing is adjusting the camber of the top wheel, just like when they set the wheels of your car to steer straight. When you move the camber in or out and the wheels spin the blade, the blade will move to the front

or rear of the tire and can walk off the tire if it is adjusted too far. In general, the idea is to keep the blade running in the center of the tire. This keeps the tension distributed evenly and the blade cutting evenly.

The tires that I mentioned are just that: rubber tires that wrap around the outside of the upper and lower wheels. These tires often have a crown, or high spot, at the center. This gives extra cushion and a slight bit of extra spring tension to the blade, but it can also make adjusting the tracking more difficult. The tires can wear out on a band saw over time, either through drying out or just through use. Keeping them clean will aid in keeping the wheels in good shape. Not to worry, though — the tires are easily replaced, and it's a whole lot like changing the tires on a bicycle. The rubber tire needs to be stretched over the rim, and sometimes that takes a little help with a screwdriver. I find it infinitely easier to change a band saw tire with the wheel off the machine. A simple nut releases the wheel from the machine.

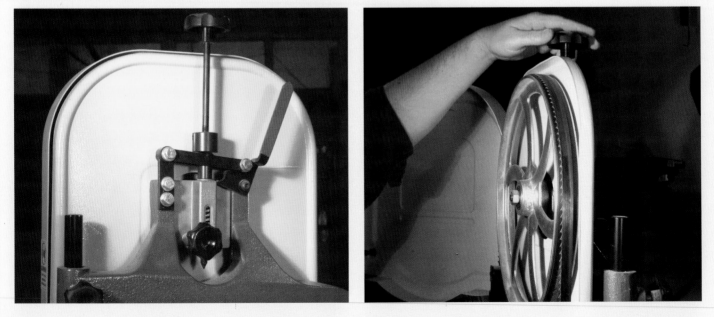

Some band saws are now equipped with a quick tension-release mechanism. The red handle shown here is just that. This is a nice addition because it makes it a simple (and amazingly quick) way to bring a blade back to the proper tension without having to turn the top tensioning knob a dozen or more times.

When you put on a new blade, or when you're using the band saw for the first time in a while, you need to properly tension the blade. The tensioning knob may be located in a few different positions, but on the average 14" (356mm) band saw (like this one) the tensioning knob is located at the top of the upper cabinet.

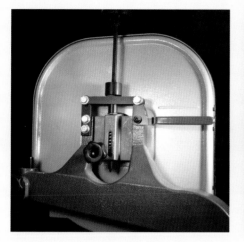

Blade tension on...

...and blade tension off. That's nice and fast and very handy.

The blade-tensioning gauge. The markings on the face of the metal relate to the width of the saw blade. By setting the tension so the marker reads at the proper blade width (sometimes tricky to determine), you're almost set. Honestly, these gauges will put you in the ballpark, but don't rely on them as dead accurate. Depending on the blade and the age/quality of your tensioning spring, you may need to tighten the tension further. As you cut it will be noticeable if the blade is too loose or slips slightly.

The knob located near the tensioning gauge is the wheel camber adjustment. It's the setting to adjust the blade tracking. Most will be set up as shown here, with a locking nut to hold the wheel in position after adjustment. This one is a wing nut, so you don't need a wrench. Thanks, Grizzly. Release the locking nut, adjust the wheel camber, then lock the nut down.

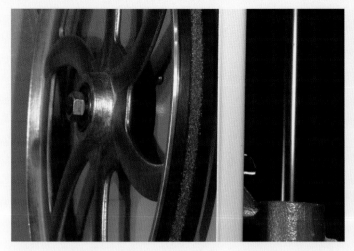

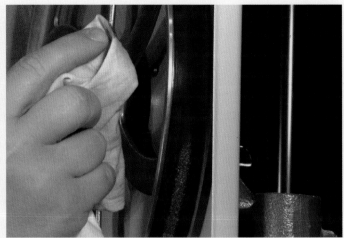

With the blade off this is a good time to check the wheel. Frequently, sawdust will become stuck to the wheel underneath the blade. Some band saws have integral brushes to clean the wheels during the saw's operation. This one doesn't on the top wheel. This buildup can cause the blade to not track properly on the crown (center) of the tire.

Clean the unwanted dirt from the tires using a brush or rag with a little mineral spirits. Don't damage the surface of the tires with overly aggressive brushing or too caustic a cleaning agent. Take this opportunity to check the tires as well. Just as with your car, the rubber will wear and with enough use will need to be replaced to ensure proper operation of the saw.

Before you take the wheels off the machine, this is a good time to check the wheel bearings. If the wheel bearings are getting worn, you won't be able to keep the blade tracking correctly. With the wheel tightened, grab the wheel in both hands and give it a shake. Too much play at the center of the wheel where it mounts to the machine will indicate bearing wear.

Happily, today's bearings are sealed and simply need to be popped loose and replaced.

As important to proper performance as the wheel alignment and tension are, the blade guides are the heart of the machine's accuracy. There are various blade guides available on different saws, but there's always a matched set: one above and one below the table surface.

In general, each guide will have some type of support mechanism on either side of the blade and a third placed behind the blade. These are known as the side guides and the thrust bearing. Follow the photos on the following pages to understand the adjustment process. Although the rear guide (the thrust bearing) is usually a bearing (clever naming, right?), the side guides

If you need to replace the tire, remove the retaining nut from the wheel and remove the wheel from the saw. Much like a bicycle tire, the tire will need to be pried from the channel in the wheel surface. A flat screwdriver will help with this operation. Putting on a new tire is reversing the action, using a screwdriver to stretch the tire over the wheel. Many manufacturers suggest wetting the new tire in water with a little dishwashing detergent added. I agree that it does make things go a little smoother. Just make sure you let the tire dry before using it.

are solid blocks or also bearings. The guide block concept is actually dated, and if you've still got guide blocks on your saw you may want to think about upgrading them to bearing guides. The bearings allow the guides to stay pretty much right up against the blade without heating the blade. This is about the most positive support you can give to a blade. A couple of other guide variations are floating around out there, but they're primarily brand specific, and until they've been around about 10 years, I'm not going to waste your time with them.

On the other hand, I do want to say a couple of things about the aging guide blocks. Though an adequate guide system, these blocks impart friction to the blade as they guide. Even though they're set to not touch the blade prior to use, once the saw's running the blade will shift and bear on the blocks. Voila, friction! It's bad for the blade and it wears the block surface, making it necessary to readjust the blocks every so often to keep the spacing tight. Originally, these guide blocks were made of steel, and a number of saws are still sold this way. New technologies, including plastics and ceramics, are replacing

the steel blocks. Either version reduces the friction and doesn't heat the blade, but the wear problem still exists. Of the two, I'd recommend ceramic.

We're down to the table now. And once again the main maintenance battle is keeping the rust off and the surface smooth. But with a band saw the table also plays a role in the machine's overall maintenance, specifically, in changing the blade. For the blade to work in a circle across the wheels, it needs to

pass through the surface of the table. This means there needs to be a hole in the table for the blade to pass through and a slot in the table to allow the blade to be removed. Maintenance becomes a bit of a ballet and it's a dance with a sharp blade, so take it easy. Take a look at the photos starting on page 59 to follow the blade changing steps, including removing the blade from the center of the table.

Something you shouldn't have to worry about, unless you're putting a lot of hours on your saw, are the wheel bearings. If the bearings begin to wear the wheel won't spin freely (with the blade removed). Bearings are usually sealed units that can be popped loose and fairly easily replaced. Again, you shouldn't have to do this, but just in case....

The upper blade-guide mechanism shown in close-up. The blade and guard are removed. These are bearing guide, which are becoming industry standards. This type of guide is replacing traditional guide block systems with good reason. Though guide

blocks function well, they wear and require frequent adjustment. They also don't let you guide the blade with direct pressure. Bearing guides allow direct pressure on the wheel and don't require frequent adjustment. By the way, these are dirty and need some quality time with a toothbrush.

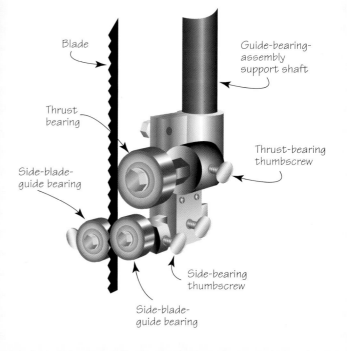

Blade

Thrust bearing

Side-blade-guide bearing

Side-blade-guide bearing

Guide-bearing-assembly support shaft

Thrust-bearing thumbscrew

Side-bearing thumbscrew

With the bearing guides properly adjusted (and the blade tracking accurately in the center of the wheel), the side view should look like this. The side guides (lower in the photo) should be set to allow the teeth on the blade to extend in front of the bearings. The thrust bearing (at top) should be set just in back of the blade (the thickness of a piece of paper) so this bearing will be contacted by the blade only when pressure is placed against the blade. This setting reduces wear on the face of the thrust bearing.

You're now ready to bring the bearings in place against the blade. Although you can allow the bearings to rest directly against the blade, I still recommend setting them just short of touching the blade (a paper's thickness as shown). The blade will still guide well and this setting will reduce some wear on the bearings. Adjust one guide first, then bring the second guide into place. Then tighten the clamping screw to lock everything in place.

Setting up the side guide bearings as seen from the front. The first step is to back the guides away from the blade. With proper blade tension applied, the blade will hang accurately across the guide assembly. If you don't back the bearings off the blade they may push the blade away from an accurate center. On this saw, backing the bearings off requires loosening the clamping screw, then rotating the bearings out of the way.

TLC time — don't neglect to take care of the top surface of the table. Keep it rust-free and add a little lubrication to keep things sliding smoothly.

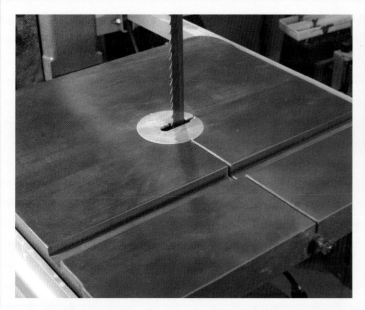

The parts of a band saw table: the table itself, the throat plate insert and the pin that keeps the table flat. To remove the blade the manufacturer has to cut a channel through the table to let the blade pass in and out of the throat area. This channel compromises the table's ability to remain in a perfectly flat plane. The pin re-aligns the table surface, holding everything flat. It's pretty important — don't lose it.

To remove the blade, first pull the pin and count to three, then throw. Just kidding — that's for hand grenades. Once again, hang on to the pin because you'll need it again. And you'll probably need a pair of pliers to get the pin out of the hole. You'll also need to pop the throat plate insert out of the way. A screwdriver will make this task easier.

With the blade tension completely released (or at least enough to allow a reasonable amount of slack in the blade) and the pin and throat plate removed, grasp the blade and guide it forward out of the upper and lower blade guides. Careful, it's still sharp. This might be a reasonable place to use gloves.

As with most woodworking machines that have a table, it's always a good idea to keep the table flat. If sawdust gets underneath the throat plate, it can sit higher than the table, causing troubles. When you've got the plate out to change the blade, use a toothbrush to clean out the rabbet the throat plate fits in.

Once free of the guides, turn the blade to align it with the channel cut in the table and slide it out of the table.

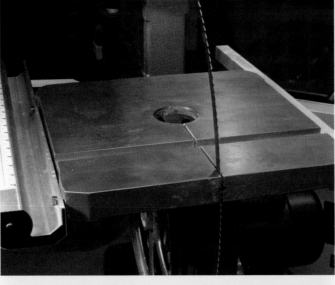

To check the center tracking on the saw you need to rotate the wheels. This is most definitely not an "under power" task. Unplug the saw and slowly turn the upper wheel by hand. Watch your fingers. If your saw has spoked wheels, as shown, you can get pinched. As you turn the wheel, adjust the wheel camber with the handle at the rear of the saw.

Now, that's a properly tracking blade. Nicely centered. Now all I have to do is get the rust off the blade!

The table is also designed to tilt. This allows for some pretty cool operations on the band saw, but that's another book — this one's about maintenance. You need to adjust the angle of the table (and the stops controlling that angle) for reliable performance. The trusty steel square is in use once again to set the stops for an accurate 90° or 45° angle on the table.

As we move below the table we get down to the lower guides and lower wheel. The maintenance on the matching units above still applies here. One thing that is a little different is the drive belt connecting the lower wheel to the motor. Check the belt for proper tension and also check it for drying, cracks or splits. If the belt's not in good shape, the saw's headed for a breakdown.

Though a band saw is one of the tools most commonly used to cut circles or curves, it still does a fair amount of straight work as well. And being able to guide a piece of wood straight through the blade is where the fence comes in. Not all band saws come equipped with fences, and when they do, they're not always the most valuable accessories. They are more of an "extra" than a standard. Hopefully, your fence locks down easily and can be locked parallel to the blade. But that's not always what you need.

Because of the way a band saw blade cuts through the wood, a situation called drift can occur. It's a reaction to the blade shape (actually the sharp square angles at the back edge of the blade) that makes you angle the wood away from parallel alignment with the blade to make a straight cut. Sounds weird, but it exists. When you're cutting freehand on the band saw it's no big deal to angle the wood to compensate for the drift. But if you're using a fence to guide the wood, you can't compensate. There are two ways to make the fence work correctly in this situation.

The first is something you can do to

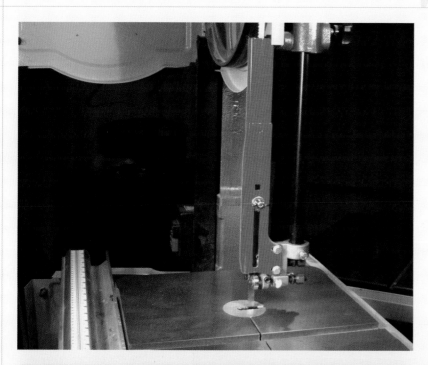

After resetting the guides (top and bottom) don't forget to put the guard back on. It may seem like an annoyance, but as with all guards, they work only if you use them. Though the band saw is a fairly easy machine to use safely, don't make it more dangerous by removing the safety gear.

A good shot of the underside of the table. Lots to take care of here, so make it easier by tipping over the table. You will be able to see and adjust the lower bearing guides more easily. And you'll need to check the beveling stops every now and again. The stop for level (0-setting, or 90° to the blade) and the 45° setting are usually a simple bolt with a stop nut. Loosen the stop nut and adjust the bolt, then tighten the stop nut and you're done. These settings may loosen up but not very often, so this is an infrequent maintenance need.

the blade itself. To "soften" the sharp edges on the rear of the saw you can actually round them slightly. This is done by rubbing a sharpening stone (though there are specific tools sold to do this job, as shown in the picture on the next page) along the back corners while the saw is running. Needless to say, this is a task to perform cautiously. This rounding of the blade will also help the blade follow nonlinear shapes, so it's a pretty good general mainte-

nance step on a brand-new saw blade. Just rounding both the back corners may solve (or at least reduce) the drift problem, but there's still one more option.

Many fences for band saws offer drift adjustment on the fence itself. Usually the screws that hold the fence to the mounting fixture attach through eccentric or elongated holes that allow you to loosen the screws and shift the angle of the fence left or right. Getting

the right angle takes a little practice. The best method I've found is to actually cut part way through a board freehand, adjusting for drift naturally by angling the board. Stop the cut in the center of the board, but leave the board laying on the saw table at the angle you had shifted. Clamp it to the table, then adjust your fence to match the edge and angle of the board. Simple, but do a couple of practice passes to check the alignment. You don't want to fight with

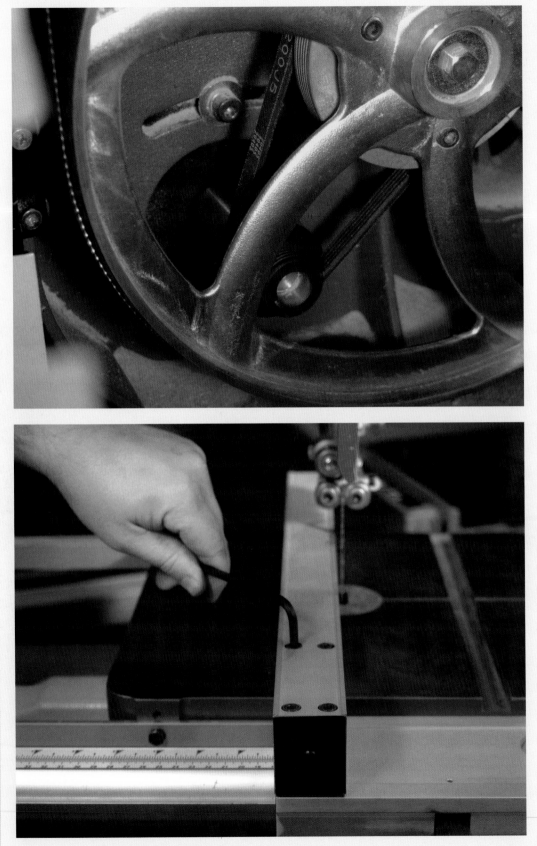

When checking the saw for dust, don't overlook the drive belt. Even though this saw uses an efficient V-belt, dust can accumulate in the ridges of the pulley and cause slipping. Keep it clean, and while you're down there, check the belt tension. It's usually a simple matter to release the motor mount bolts and add a little extra tension on the belt.

One of the idiosyncrasies of band saws is something called drift. Because of the way blades are manufactured, it's often necessary to angle the wood as it feeds into the blade to make a straight cut. That's easy enough to deal with when cutting freehand, but if your saw is equipped with a fence, drift can cause you to fight with the material feed. If you're lucky, your band saw fence will allow you to adjust the fence to allow for drift. Check the manual. Otherwise, you may need to shim the fence to compensate.

or bind the blade.

One final, but important topic: the blades themselves. There are so many brands of band saw blades available that their discussion could easily be a chapter on its own. Use your common sense. If it's a very affordable blade it's not likely to hold an edge as long as a more pricey blade. The angle and spacing of the teeth are job specific and there are many variations, but again, to keep it simple, the fewer teeth per inch on the blade the more aggressive and the faster the cut. The tooth angle

(or rake) will also impact the speed and quality of cut. The more aggressive the rake, the faster the cut. But, the more aggressive and faster the cut, the less clean the cut will be. The blade will leave rippled edges on the wood making more clean up necessary before use. Lots of teeth indicate a blade that will leave a cleaner cut, but it will cut slower.

Also, the wider the blade, the easier it will be to cut straight (follow the cut) in the wood. For tighter circles and radii, a thinner blade is the way to go.

Some blades are made with a special steel alloy that allow them to run under less tension and still track well in a cut. These "Swedish steel" blades may sound like some kind of black magic, but they're actually very good in a cut and I'd recommend you try one on your saw for improved performance.

That's the band saw. Lots of parts and many things to keep an eye on. Keeping a band saw properly tuned can be a love/hate relationship, but when it's working well, the band saw is a great tool and a pleasure to use.

Band Saw Blade-Selection Chart

Hardwoods

RADIUS OF CUT	MATERIAL THICKNESS	BLADE WIDTH X TPI
3/8"	0 - 2½"	3/16" x 10
5/8"	0 - 3/4"	1/4" x 10
	3/4" - 1½"	1/4" x 8
	1½" - 2½"	1/4" x 6
	2½" - 6"	1/4" x 4
1¼"	0 - 3/4"	3/8" x 10
	3/4" - 1½"	3/8" x 8
	1½" - 2½"	3/8" x 6
	2½" - 6"	3/8" x 4
2½"	0 - 3/4"	1/2" x 10
	3/4" - 1½"	1/2" x 8
	1½" - 2½"	1/2" x 6
	2½" - 6"	1/2" x 4
5½"	0 - 3/4"	3/4" x 10
	3/4" - 1½"	3/4" x 8
	1½" - 2½"	3/4" x 6
	2½" - 6"	3/4" x 4
7"	0 - 3/4"	1" x 10
	3/4" - 1½"	1" x 8
	1½" - 2½"	1" x 6
	2½" - 6"	1" x 4

Softwoods

RADIUS OF CUT	MATERIAL THICKNESS	BLADE WIDTH X TPI
3/8"	0 - 1½"	3/16" x 10
5/8"	0 - 1/2"	1/4" x 10
	1/2" - 1"	1/4" x 8
	1" - 1½"	1/4" x 6
	1½" - 4"	1/4" x 4
1¼"	0 - 1/2"	3/8" x 10
	1/2" - 1"	3/8" x 8
	1" - 1½"	3/8" x 6
	1½" - 4"	3/8" x 4
2½"	0 - 1/2"	1/2" x 10
	1/2" - 1"	1/2" x 8
	1" - 1½"	1/2" x 6
	1½" - 4"	1/2" x 4
5½"	0 - 1/2"	3/4" x 10
	1/2" - 1"	3/4" x 8
	1" - 1½"	3/4" x 6
	1½" - 4"	3/4" x 4
7"	0 - 1/2"	1" x 10
	1/2" - 1"	1" x 8
	1" - 1½"	1" x 6
	1½" - 4"	1" x 4

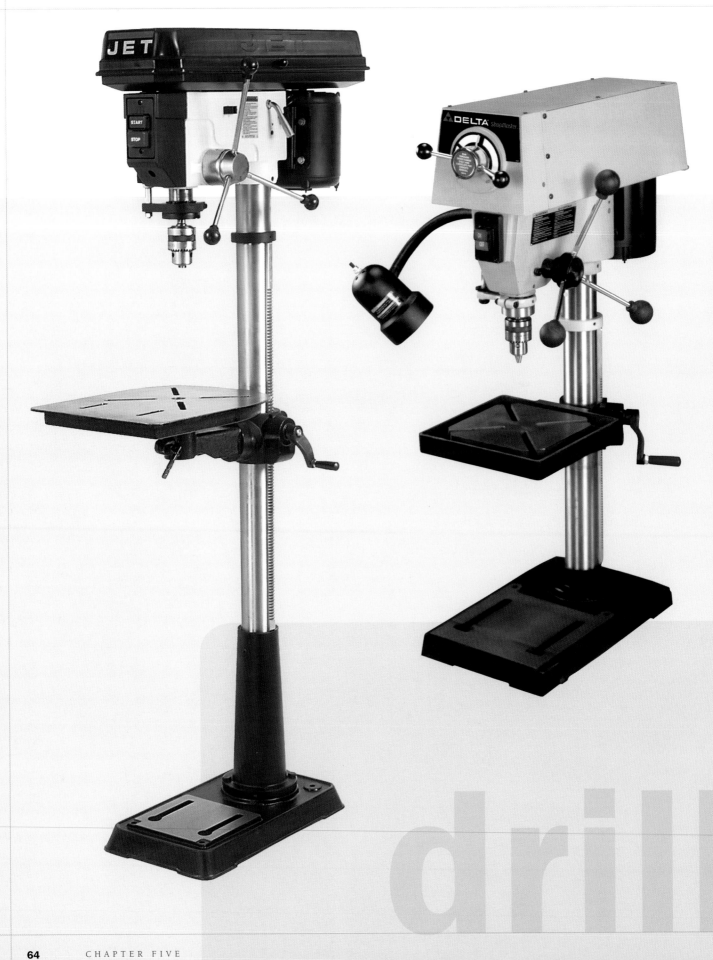

drill presses

WELCOME TO THE CHAPTER dedicated to the drill press… or the "drill-on-a-stick" chapter. When you think about it, that's all a drill press is. The only thing that a drill press does better than a drill is allow you to drill perfectly straight holes over and over again without worrying about it.

And, of course, a drill press requires less physical energy. Because of the gearing involved in the quill assembly, you can put much more force behind the bit by pulling down on the handle than you'll be able to do by leaning in behind a handheld drill.

Well, wait a drill press is also pretty efficient at making repeated accurate holes at angles as well. Because the table will tilt, a variety of angles are possible. This is a valuable tool for chairmakers who need to make accurate sockets for chair spindles.

Although the drill press is a fixture in most woodworking shops, this machine was born in the metalmilling industry. It was the answer to making lots of accurate holes without worrying about human error, or human boredom. If you had to drill the same hole in the same place all day long, you'd lose your mind and almost certainly turn out less-than-perfect results on the one thousandth hole.

Another advantage to a drill press is the ability to accurately control the speed of the bit. Different diameter cutting tools operated more efficiently at different speeds. Though you can slow down the revolutions per minute on a drill by squeezing the trigger a little less (if it's a variable-speed drill), it's hardly accurate.

The belt and pulley system on a drill presses allows you to accurately set the speed that's best for the bit you're using — better for the hole and certainly better for the bit.

Types

There are two main categories of drill presses: benchtop and stationary. The only difference is the length of the column supporting the head and motor. Yes, you can drill into a 30"-long (762mm) table leg on a stationary drill press but not so easily on a benchtop. But how often do you do that? In general, if most of your drill press work is performed flat, you're better off using the space under the drill press for something other than a longer column.

Beyond benchtop or stationary, drill presses are sold by the inch and motor size. Oddly, the inch size related to drill presses doesn't make sense in my book. A 12" (305mm) drill press means you can drill a hole in the center of a 12" (305mm) piece of wood. What seems easier to define is that the drilling center of the bit is positioned 6" (152mm) from the column. Whatever. At least you'll know what you're shopping for. Drill presses are available in 8" (203mm) to 20" (508mm) and larger configurations and can range in price from $80 to $800 or more. Honestly, most drill presses are created pretty close to equal. It's not an overly complicated machine, with the greater variables falling in the motor performance and the accuracy afforded. As always, you get what you pay for, so shoot comfortably in the middle of the pack and buy the features you need.

Parts

We've adapted this metal-working tool to woodworking, but we've made some compromises along the way. Drilling into metal requires different speeds at

Proper performance on a drill press is often determined by using the machine at the proper speed. In the vast majority of drill presses, the speed is controlled by the belt-and-pulley arrangement. By adjusting the position of the belts on the pulleys you raise or lower the spindle speed. As for maintenance, the pulleys spin on bearings, but you really need to use your drill press a lot to ever have to worry about the bearings going. More important, check to keep things clean (not too much dust) and greased. Also check the belts for wear and cracking.

the bit than drilling in wood (metal requires slower speeds). Because of this, drill presses have adjustable speeds, usually accomplished by a confusing array of pulley and belt adjustments. And because it's confusing and awkward, most woodworkers don't change the speeds, and we burn up tooling and wood along the way.

Another leftover metal-working tradition is the table. These iron tables were designed for milling metal, even offering drainage channels for cutting oil. They don't offer convenient clamp-

ing or indexing means, and not even a fence, which is an important measuring and safety feature for a woodworker. Most woodworkers end up making their own auxiliary fence-and-table system, and I recommend that approach. Dozens of plans are available in magazines and online for an adequate answer to the metal-working table:

- DIYData.com (www.diydata.com)
- Bob's Plans (www.bobsplans.com)
- Popular Woodworking magazine (www.popularwoodworking.com)

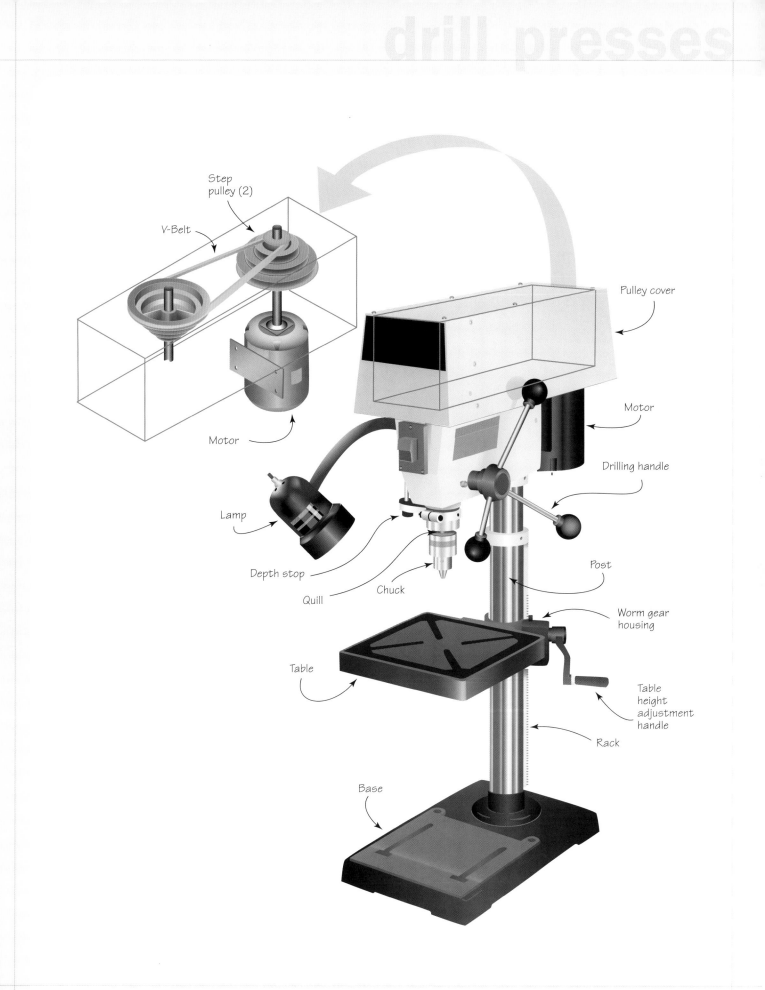

Step pulley (2)

V-Belt

Pulley cover

Motor

Motor

Drilling handle

Lamp

Depth stop

Quill

Chuck

Post

Worm gear housing

Table

Table height adjustment handle

Rack

Base

Drill Bit Speed Chart (FOR DRILL PRESSES)

Bit Type	Material			
TWIST/BRAD	SOFTWOODS	HARDWOODS	ALUMINUM/BRASS	MILD STEEL
	RPM	RPM	RPM	RPM
Point Bit				
1/16" - 3/16"	2500	2200	1250	1700
1/4" - 3/8"	1900	1700	1000	1250
7/16" - 3/4"	1000	1000	700	800
Spade/Forstner				
3/8" - 5/8"	2000	1600	NA	NA
11/16" -1"	1200	1000	NA	NA
11/16" -1 7/16"	800	600	NA	NA
2"- 3"	500	450	NA	NA
Hole Saws				
1/2" - 3/4"	500	500	650	500
1" -1 3/4"	300	300	300	250
2" -2 1/2"	200	200	200	170
3"- 4"	100	100	100	100
5"	75	75	75	75

Maintenance

Let's start with the confusing part. These aren't so much maintenance tasks as daily smarter-way-of-working tasks. To begin with, set the drill press speed correctly for the task. First you need to know what the proper speed is. I've made this easy by including a chart above.

Now you know the speed you're shooting for, but you need to figure out how the belts should be arranged to accomplish that speed. Open the pulley cover on your drill press and take a look inside. Most drill presses have three cone-shaped step pulleys inside, two pointing up and one pointing down, each with grooves to hold the belts. There should be a chart mounted inside the cover, or possibly in your owner's manual, that will tell you the proper belt/pulley arrangement to reach your required speed setting. Once

you've got that, you need to move the belts.

The front pulley is fixed in place and connects directly to the quill and chuck on the machine. The center pulley is freefloating and is tensioned as the belts are tightened. The rear pulley, connected to the motor, is the pulley that directly affects the belt tension. Loosen the motor mounts (one or two screws or bolts, depending on your machine) and the motor will move freely toward the front of the machine and release the tension on all the belts. Rearrange the belts to match the recommended speed, then tension and tighten the rear pulley and motor. Not so bad, is it? But if you'd rather avoid this step altogether, a few drill press models on the market allow you to adjust the quill speed on the fly with one handle. This is a great feature that gives you one less argument for not setting

the machine to the proper speed. In my book (Hey, that's this one here!), I recommend spending the extra money for this convenience.

Let's look at the rest of the moving parts. The table moves in a couple of ways, and each needs to be checked for smooth operation. To adjust the table height there is a geared crank to move the table with less stress — that is, if the gearing and toothed guide are properly aligned and maintained. A loose or misaligned guide track can make moving the table up and down a chore rather than an operation. Check this setup in your owner's manual, but in general, straight and snug is good. Make sure the gearing has a little lubrication on it to help the metal-to-metal operation. Surface rust on the column or around the table mount can slow things down. Light sanding and lubrication will also help on the column. (If you're using the existing metal table, keep it rust-free and oiled as well.) Once the proper table height is achieved, remember to lock the table in place. Not only is this safer, it keeps the quill and clearance hole in the table aligned, and it maintains the right-angle orientation of the quill to the table.

Your drill press table is also capable of some rotation from the standard horizontal (90° quill-to-table) position. In most cases this is a 45° rotation, but some will move all the way to a vertical position, which is nice. In any case, the table will have some type of mechanism to preset the stopping point at the horizontal, vertical or 45° location. Use a combination square and/or engineer's square to determine the proper position, then lock in that setting on the table stops. If your machine includes a scale to adjust the table, check it against your accurate settings to determine if you can rely on the scale for settings between the set stops.

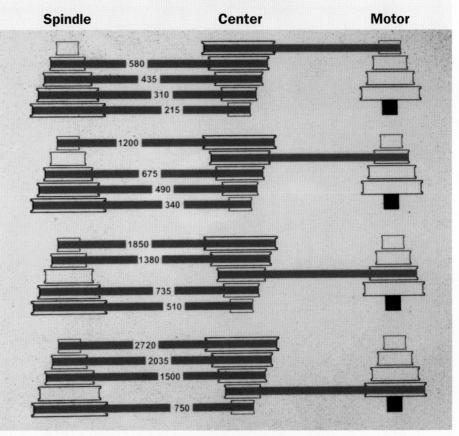

SPINDLE SPEEDS

Spindle   Center   Motor

580
435
310
215

1200
675
490
340

1850
1380
735
510

2720
2035
1500
750

Your particular machine will have information on how to set the belts and pulleys for the proper speed. That information is often mounted in the lid with the pulleys. All you need to know is the best speed for the particular bit you're using. The attached chart on the previous page will help with that.

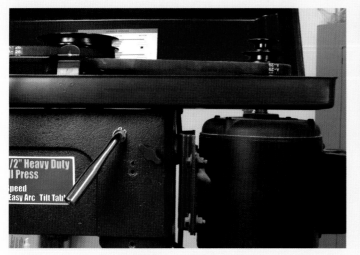

To adjust the quill speed, the belts need to be loosened. Fairly typical on drill presses are a tensioning handle and motor position-locking screws (often one on either side of the press head). After releasing the screws, the motor will slip toward the front of the machine because of the pressure of the belts. After you reposition the belts, the tensioning handle is moved to the rear of the machine, pushing the motor back and applying tension to the belts. If you don't have a tensioning lever, a stout piece of scrap wood will allow you to lever the motor away from the housing. Then reset first one and then both of the locking screws.

To raise and lower the height of the table is a geared handle that tracks in a toothed track affixed to the side of the post. If your drill press has been set up correctly, the toothed track is fitted between an upper and lower capture ring that allows the track to rotate around the post as the table is moved. This process works if the capture rings are clean and free from dirt. Also, a liberal amount of grease or lubricant on the post and the track will make the movement of the table smoother, if not easy.

Almost every drill press table will pivot to at least 45°. Some will pivot all the way to the vertical position, as does the one shown here. The fortunate few offer positive stops, as shown. Most include only a stop screw and locking lever, not that there's anything wrong with that. Most of your drill press work will likely take place with the table in the horizontal position, but you should take the time to set the angle stops so that you can set the table without putting a square against the quill every time. As with any mechanism, less dust and a little grease will keep things moving easier.

Look at that surface rust starting to form on the post! Glad it's not my drill press. This machine allows you to tip the table to either the right or the left of the post. Most will allow only a single direction. This is also an upgraded machine — it has a scale to show the angle location of the table. Many drill presses don't include this feature. Even with the scale, take the time to check the angle in a couple of locations to confirm the accuracy of the scale.

As you can see in the photo, using a drill bit to help with this setup makes things easier. You can also see that squaring the table works in more than the side-to-side relationship. It's important to check the angle the bit is drilling in all aspects. Otherwise, you might as well just use a corded drill.

One of the valuable features on any drill press is the depth stop. Some are fairly simple but effective. Others are more involved and even more effective. The stop on the drill press shown on the next page is two-fold and provides accurate depth adjustment in an easy-to-use method. As for maintenance, the only real concern, once again, is keeping the dust from gumming up the works.

As with a handheld drill, the chuck is the place where the bit hits the wood, and on a drill press, it's also where things can go wrong. On initial set-up of your machine you were most likely asked to install the chuck and quill to the machine. In about 99 percent of the drill presses in existence that attachment is a pressure fit, with the tapered quill seating into a matching column. The tapering is designed to lock the chuck and quill in perfect alignment so there is no concern of an eccentric chuck. If for some reason you're getting some run-out on your chuck, your first check should be to see if the bit is bent. Simply remove it from the chuck and roll it on a flat surface. If it rolls evenly, the bit's probably okay. It's not quite a scientific test, but it still works.

If your bit is straight and you chuck it into the machine to ensure proper alignment and you still get a wobble, the chuck may have shifted on the quill. It's fairly simple to remove the quill. While it's free of the machine, take the opportunity to check the chuck for dust and ease of movement. A little grease on the accessible moving parts won't hurt either. Then, replace the chuck using either of the methods shown in the photos on the following pages.

It's easy to forget general maintenance on a drill press. We don't use the machine all that often, and when we do it's usually a pretty quick task. Because there are so few things to actually worry about to keep things running smoothly, take the time now and again to spruce it up, and it'll be ready for those quick tasks with little setup time.

About squaring the table... it's fairly simple to adjust the table pivot. Install a good-sized bit in the chuck (make sure it's not bent and that it seats well against the chuckjaws) and use a square to check the relationship to the table. Simple. Unfortunately, the relationship shown in the photo isn't from left-to-right but from front-to-back. Someone's been a little tough on this table and actually bent it out of square. You've got two options here: Either shim the table mounting against the post, or bend it back. I recommend some gentle but persuasive taps with a dead-blow hammer.

A closer look at the depth stop shows another nice feature on this model. Rotating the black knob moves the depth stop up and down in a measured (and measurable) manner, making fine adjustments easy. But if you need to move the stop an inch or two at a time, the button in the center of the stop allows you to bypass the teeth on the rod and move the stop quickly — a nice time-saving feature. Keep it clean and lubed.

Keeping the chuck operating smoothly on a drill press is a lot like chuck maintenance on a drill — keep the dust out and add a little lubricant every now and then. On occasion, there are reasons to remove the chuck from the quill — for cleaning and to reseat the chuck to correct any centering issues. Some machines offer a chuck-release access hole in the quill, as shown here. Others don't and require a more crude approach. If you don't find this access slot in the quill, you'll need to take that dead-blow hammer and lightly tap the top of the chuck on opposite sides, working in a repeating 12:00, 6:00, 3:00 and 9:00 pattern until the chuck falls free.

All drill presses will have some type of depth stop. Some are easier to use than others. This machine offers one (actually two) that I find very useful. Shown at the left is a depth stop that can be dialed in to set a fairly accurate setting. But the feature that I like on this machine is the blue locking stud on the right. You can lower the head to the required depth, then lock this stud in place, freezing the head. Then you can set the adjustable depth stop on the right. Without this locking stud you have to deal with a lot of trial and error.

If you've got the access hole, a stout screwdriver placed in the hole and levered against the top of the quill will pop the chuck assembly free.

With the chuck assembly free you can do basic maintenance on the chuck. Also, check the quill for any rust or gouging that might affect the fit. Sandpaper and basic rust removing will take care of things here.

Different manufacturers recommend varying methods of reinserting the chuck assembly. Many tell you to slip the quill into place, then give it a couple of taps with a mallet. That works.

I prefer a more gentle method that uses the pressure of the drill press. Adjust the table to a few inches below the bottom of the positioned quill and place a scrap of wood on the table. Then lower the drill head with the handle, bringing the chuck into contact with the wood. Give it a little extra pressure once or twice and the chuck will be seated.

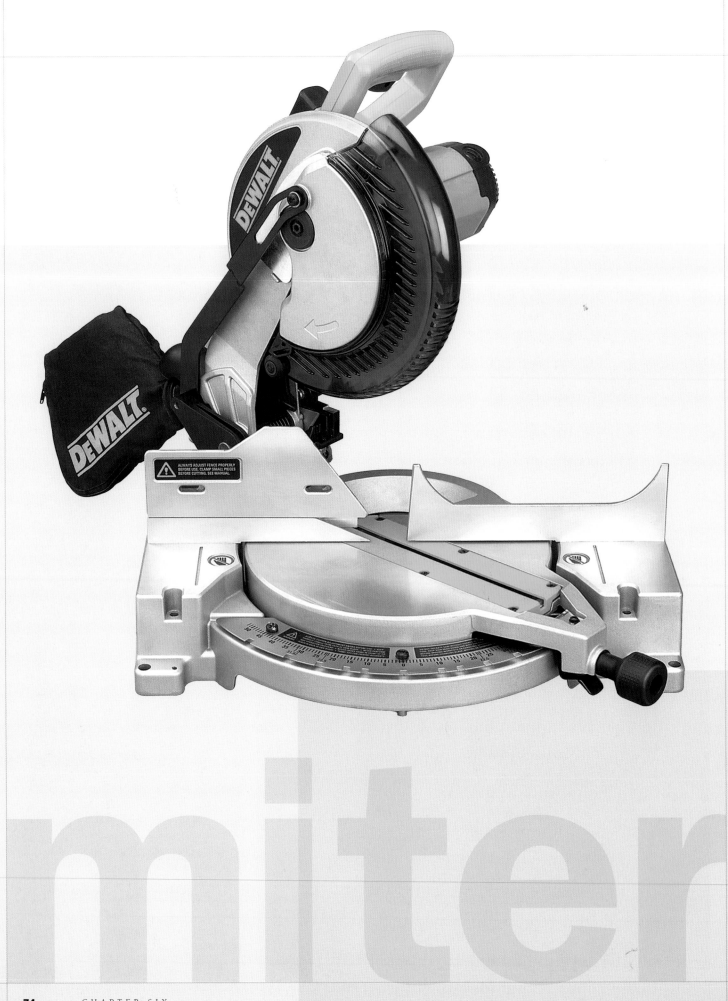

miter saws

BY VOLUME, THE MITER SAW is probably the second most-often sold tool, right behind the drill. Part of the reasoning behind this growth is the decline of the radial-arm saw and the rapid improvements that have been made to miter saws over the past 15 years. Though many a woodworker still happily uses his radial-arm saw, if you're shopping for a cut-off machine, radial-arm saws are expensive. They also take up a fair amount of space and can be difficult to keep accurate.

Conversely, the basic miter saw evolved into the compound miter saw and then the sliding compound miter saw, adding impressive capacity, portability, reasonable economies of scale and reliable accuracy. If you already own a radial-arm saw, you don't need to replace it with a miter saw, but a miter saw will likely make a strong companion to your radial-arm.

Miter saws are used extensively in carpentry, and many of them spend more time in the back of a van or pick-up on the way to a job site than they do in shops. But their convenience and capabilities make them an excellent woodworking tool as well. Whether cutting miters or compound miters on mouldings for a project or just crosscutting a number of pieces that need to be the same length (and square!), the miter saw is a great tool to have around.

Types

Miter saws are available in three significant designs: standard, compound and sliding. On a standard miter saw the blade pivots left-to-right to cut miters. A compound miter saw adds the ability to tip, or bevel, the blade either to the left or the right, though there are compound saws that will bevel in both directions. This allows you to miter and bevel during the same cut, making… you guessed it, a compound miter. Sliding miter saws are compound miter saws that have extension rails added that allow the blade and motor to slide forward and back, increasing the width of cut possible on the machine, though the cutting action remains the same as with a compound miter saw.

Prices for these saws range from under $100 to over $600 — quite a range. To be perfectly honest with you, those three categories should probably be reduced to two, because it's significantly harder to find a standard miter saw. If you can buy a compound miter saw with greater capabilities for the same price as a standard miter saw, why wouldn't you? Thus, standard miter saws are disappearing from the store shelves.

So, narrowing our conversation to compound and sliding compound miter saws, let's talk for a second on why to choose one over the other. Both of these saw styles are available with 8" (203mm), 10" (254mm) and 12" (305mm) blades, with 10" (254mm) and 12" (305mm) models being the most popular. The different blade sizes equate to different cut capacities, which is the significant factor in choosing between a compound or sliding compound saw.

Capacities are usually given at both 90°/90° and at 45°/45°, meaning, with the blade straight ahead and straight up and down, and with the blade beveled and mitered to 90° or 45° for a full compound miter cut. There are lots of stops in the middle of these two extremes and ways to combine the

two, but it's a good way to evaluate the saw's capacity in a hurry. The number will vary slightly from manufacturer to manufacturer, but these numbers from Makita's miter saw category will give you a good idea of the capacities.

10" (254mm) compound miter:
90°/90° - $2^3/4$" × $5^1/8$"-wide (70mm × 130mm)
45°/45° - $1^5/8$" × $3^5/8$"-wide (35mm × 92mm)

12" (305mm) compound miter:
90°/90° - $3^7/8$" × 6"-wide (98mm × 152mm)
45°/45° - $1^3/4$" × $5^1/2$"-wide (45mm × 140mm)

10" (254mm) sliding compound miter:
90°/90° - $3^5/8$" × 12"-wide (92mm × 305mm)
45°/45° - 2" × $8^3/4$"-wide (51mm × 222mm)

12" sliding compound miter:
90°/90° - $3^7/8$" × $12^1/4$"-wide (98mm × 311mm)
45°/45° - $2^3/16$" × $8^5/8$"-wide (56mm × 219mm)

The capacity gain between 10" (254mm) and 12" (305mm) compound miter saws is not large, but there is a gain with only a reasonable increase in price. When you move into the sliding compound category the capacities increase rapidly, nearly doubling the width of cut possible. Of course, the price nearly doubles as well.

The other significant difference between these saws will be the motor size. They're all equipped with universal motors designed for short, fast bursts of speed, and that's exactly what you need in a miter saw — probably the best use of that motor design in any woodworking tool. Motor sizes range from 12 to 15 amps, which isn't a huge spread. The motor capacity isn't usually a huge factor in a purchase, but given the option, a 15-amp saw would be a

good choice.

If you're shopping for a miter saw for woodworking needs, I'd recommend a 10" (254mm) sliding compound model, if you can swing the price. The extra capacity will come in handy, and the increase to a 12" (305mm) slider will cost you more with only a slight increase in capacity. Oh, and the 12" (305mm) blades are more expensive. For most woodworking the 10" (254mm) slider will cover your needs.

One thing I want to mention here is the introduction of laser guides on miter saws. These have become almost universal on miter saws these days, but it's my opinion that their popularity has less to do with increased accuracy and more about marketing and keeping up with the competition. A few different styles of lasers are available: single or double lasers, lasers that are on with the flip of a switch and others that light only when the blade is spinning. My recommendation is a dual laser (show both sides of the blade) and a model that is on without the blade spinning. Most are adjustable and are reasonably reliable. It will depend on your work style whether a laser is a benefit to your accuracy. But I wouldn't buy a miter saw because of its laser. Just my two cents.

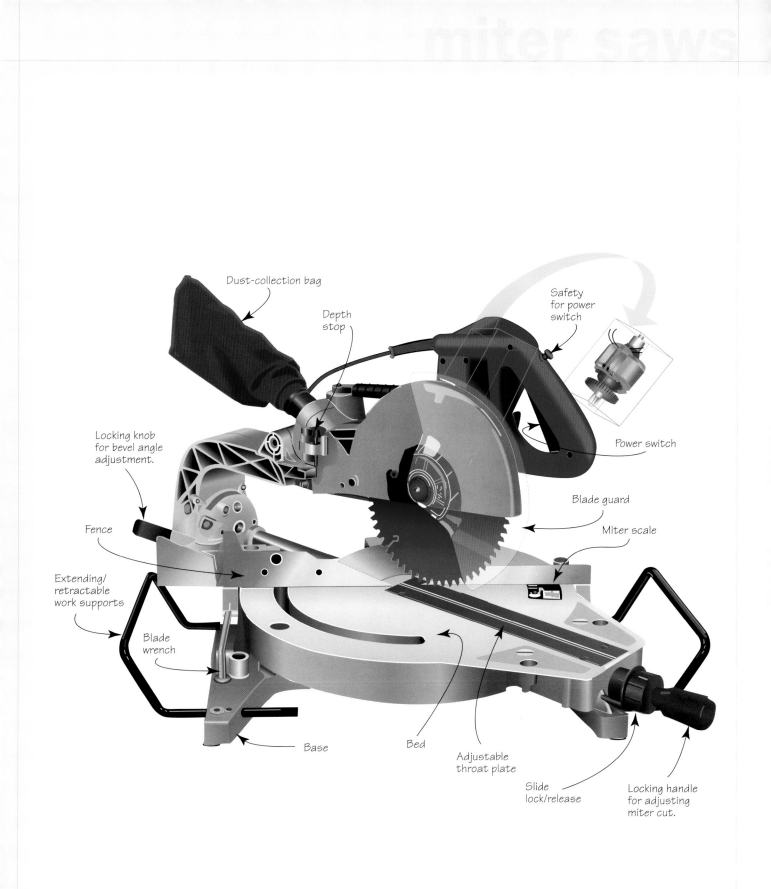

Dust-collection bag

Depth stop

Safety for power switch

Locking knob for bevel angle adjustment.

Power switch

Fence

Blade guard

Miter scale

Extending/ retractable work supports

Blade wrench

Base

Bed

Adjustable throat plate

Slide lock/release

Locking handle for adjusting miter cut.

To change the blade, the first step is to get the guard out of the way. I find a squeeze clamp works well. Then, release the bolt (or bolts) holding the access plate in place.

With the access plate swung out of the way, the blade bolt is easy to reach. But pay attention to those stickers on the saw! Miter saw blade bolts are reverse threaded, so lefty-loosey isn't going to work.

Maintenance

Taking care of your miter saw is mostly about keeping it accurate. A sharp blade (and the correct blade) doesn't hurt either. Remember, for a cleaner, slower cut, use a blade with lots of teeth. For a quicker, rougher cut, fewer teeth will do. And because we're talking about the blade, let's talk about changing the blade and what maintenance is possible during that process.

Every manufacturer has a slightly different method to change the blade, but most of the time you need to get the guard out of the way, remove a cover over the blade mount and take off the nut. The photos on these pages show this process on a Makita. With the blade removed, we have our first opportunity for maintenance and a chance to keep things accurate. Dust builds up in a miter saw. The obligatory attached dust bag may collect half of the dust. I highly recommend attaching a shop vacuum to your miter saw for a more pleasant work environment. The dust in and around the blade mount can affect performance. A blade needs to spin straight, and any dust or crud built up on either of the washer plates supporting the blade can slightly affect the spin of the blade. While you've got the blade off, take a few seconds to check the washers and clean off any debris. Let's face it, if you added a laser to a saw to increase the accuracy, having the width of the kerf affected by a slightly wobbling blade doesn't make sense. Keep it clean.

Another quality-of-cut issue that can be addressed at (well, near) the blade is tear-out. Because of the way a miter saw blade cuts, the underside of the board (the side lying on the table) is most prone to tear-out. Every miter saw has a replaceable throat plate in the table, just like a table saw. On all but the least expensive miter saws, this throat plate can be adjusted to leave a smaller opening to help reduce tear-out. Lots of miter saw owners don't bother to adjust this opening. That's

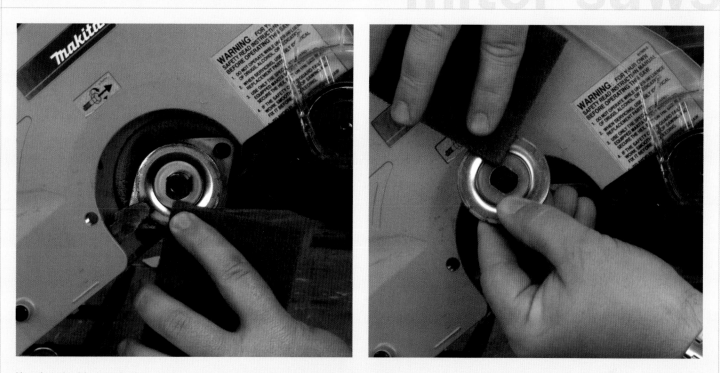

Keeping the blade spinning straight is pretty easy. Check both the mounting plate and the washer for dust buildup or rust. A synthetic scouring pad will knock down any high spots that could affect the blade's spin.

sometimes understandable because if you make a beveled cut with the saw, the throat plate needs to be widened to accommodate the angled blade. Often, the throat plate opening gets "adjusted" by the blade itself widening the kerf during a cut. But it's worth training yourself to adjust the throat plate opening to reduce that tear-out. Hey, it's less time sanding! What other excuse do you need?

And while we're playing around with the table, let's talk about keeping it clean too. It's rare to find anything but an aluminum miter saw table. Luckily, that means you won't have to worry about rust, but it's always a good idea to keep the dust off it. Although I usually recommend a little lubricant on a tabletop, I'm not going to do that here. The table surfaces are usually pretty slick anyway, and more often, as you make a cut, the rotation of the blade has a tendency to try to move the board a little. The trick on a miter saw is keeping the material in place during the cut, not keeping it sliding. So keep the wax off this table.

While we're looking at the tabletop,

If your saw comes equipped with an adjustable throat plate, use it! It's a simple way to reduce tear-out on the back of your material. But also remember to reset the throat opening when you make a bevel cut. The kerf will need to be wider to accommodate the blade angle.

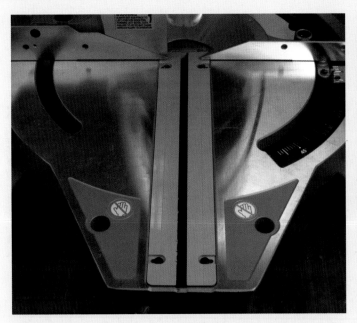

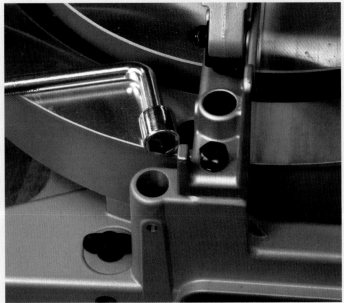

Two features I find attractive in a miter saw are a generously sized table surface and an easily read scale. The scales aren't usually adjustable, but take the time to identify how accurate yours is. And remember, no lubricant on that generous table! Also, take a look at the fence in this photo. Two fences, left and right, connected in the middle by a half-moon section of aluminum. If that extrusion is bent you're going to have a bear of a time setting the fences accurately.

Adjusting the fence square to the blade, or to shim underneath, requires releasing the hold-down bolts. The fence may be of a one-piece or a two-piece design. The two-piece is easier to adjust.

let's talk about the fence for a minute. When you're talking about accuracy, the fence is the first place to start. Most fences on miter saws are a single aluminum extrusion running the width of the saw table. The fence face doesn't run the entire length but rather it's divided at the blade with what amounts to a connector. So essentially you've got two fences that are locked together. This arrangement can make it easy to adjust both fences perpendicular to the blade while still being in alignment with one another... unless your fence is bent. Some saws offer independent fences, which I prefer, but these one-piece fences are the standard, so take it easy with them.

To align the fences with the blade you want to start on one side of the blade. Bring the blade down into the table and lock it in that position. Get your engineer's square and place it in the angle created by the fence and the blade. Loosen the hold-down bolts on the entire fence and get the one side

accurate. Lock in that side, then switch to the other side of the blade to check the other fence. If it's square, leave it alone and lift the blade out of the table. Use a straightedge to confirm that the two fence sides are in line with one another, then tighten the bolts on the second side of the fence. If things are out of square or out of alignment and you have a single-piece fence, you can tweak the fence a little to bring things in line. But be careful, because aluminum is brittle and I've seen a couple of fences snap during "adjusting."

That's only one adjustment for the fences. We also need to make sure they're square to the table. Why? Because the thickness of material you're cutting on the saw will vary and we want to make sure that both fences will hold any thickness material accurately aligned across the width of the table. Because you've still got your engineer's square handy, place it in the corner formed by the fence and the table and check it for square. You'll

need to check along the length of the fence in a few locations to make sure there's no twist in the fence. Check the fence while it's tightened down, because even that process could twist a fence out of square.

Your next adjustment is getting the blade square to the table. On the Makita, the blade bevels by releasing a knob at the rear of the saw. But that's just to bevel the saw, not to square it. With the bevel set at 90°, grab your square again and fit it into the corner created by the blade and the table. Once again, check your position against the body of the saw, not the teeth. If you're not square, you'll need to adjust the 90° stop on the saw. For this model that adjustment is located at the rear of the saw again. Sneak up on your adjustment, then lock it in.

If you have your miter saw set up in a stationary location, you may have to check the bevel and miter adjustments only a couple of times a year. On the other hand, if you're moving your saw

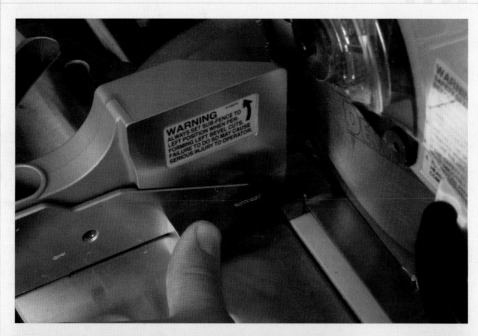

Getting the fences square to the blade requires the engineer's square once again. When squaring against the blade, work from the surface of the body, not from the teeth. It's more accurate this way.

Squaring the fence to the table may not be important in rough carpentry, but as a woodworker it is. A flashlight behind the square will quickly point out any gap. Miter saws don't allow any way to adjust the fence face to square with the table, but you can shim the fence. Tape is fine for a temporary shim, but a metal shim (brass shimming material is available at automotive stores) will wear longer. A little spray adhesive on the back and the fence will always be accurate.

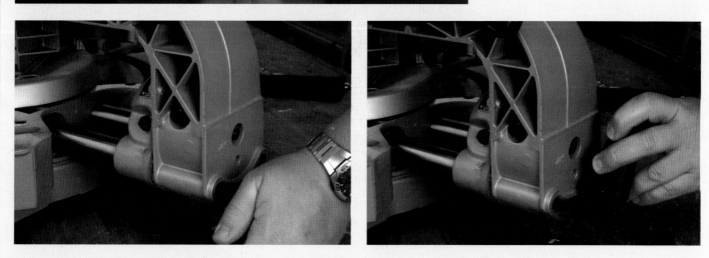

The majority of miter saws have their bevel-lock knob at the rear of the saw. Some are knobs; others are levers, as shown here. A quarter-turn of the lever releases the saw housing.

When aligning the blade's vertical adjustment, a square is indispensable, but a flashlight can be pretty helpful as well. By shining the light from behind the square, it's very easy to see the blade is offset from 90°.

When adjusting the vertical blade setting, the bevel stops are important. By releasing the stop bolts the blade can be set perfectly vertical. Then, ease the stops into place and tighten. This saw is a single bevel. If you have a dual bevel saw (beveling to either side) you'll have two 45° stops to set.

from location to location and tossing it in your truck more often than not, you may want to check these settings much more often.

There's only one more setting to concern yourself with, and I've know woodworkers who have never bothered to use this setting. The depth setting isn't for general use but rather for cutting dadoes in material, and because of that, it's a setting you'll most commonly find only on sliding compound saws. You can set the stop to cut at a variety of depths, and most of the depth mechanisms allow you to set the depth and then engage or disengage the stop for quick use.

Mechanically, you may have to check you brushes for wear over time, and a little lubricant on the blade pivot mechanism might be necessary once a year. And, of course, check the cord for cracks of breaks, but other than that, a miter saw is really designed to stand up to abuse and need very little care. What a nice tool!

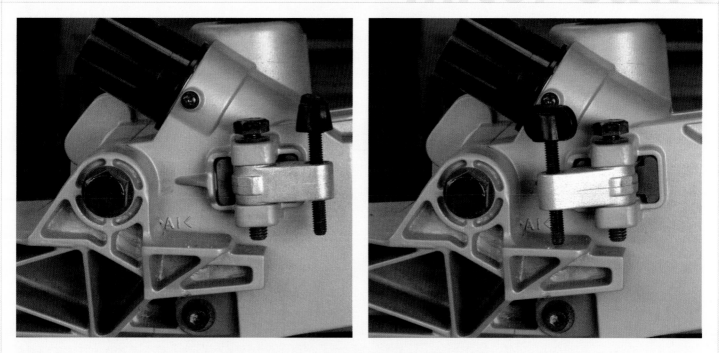

Sliding miter saws can be used to create dadoes. By setting the cut-depth gauge you can simply adjust the saw to cut dadoes from above with multiple passes. Even more simple, this saw allows you to keep the setting but swing the gauge out of the way when not needed.

The brushes aren't always this easy to access on all miter saws. There's still plenty of life left on this guy and it's wearing evenly, so this motor's in good shape.

routers

ROUTERS ARE ONE OF MY FAVORITE power tools. I think it's because you can do so many things with them and it all fits in the palm of your hand. Whether it's joinery (from rabbets to dovetails) or some really cool edge profiles for mouldings, routers are just amazingly capable.

Routers are great because you can do so many things with them. Whether it's joinery (from rabbets to dovetails) or some really cool edge profiles for mouldings, routers are just amazingly versatile. You can use a trim router that fits in the palm of your hand for dozens of applications. Or you can opt for a larger fixed-base or plunge router for more strenuous work. And with a little work in the shop you can mount any router into a router table for another couple of dozen applications, even making your own frame and panel doors.

One of the newest additions to the router world is the multibase router. Sometimes a fixed-base router is preferable over a plunge router. In other instances, the converse is true. Now, rather than having to buy two routers, you can purchase one router motor with two bases! Very cool.

What Is a Router?

Well, it's our old friend the universal motor attached to something called a collet, which holds the bit. Collets are unique to router-type tools (rotary tools like Dremels also use collets). It's a sectioned collar with fingers that grab the bit by tightening a nut on the fingers. It's a good hold, and that's a good thing because routers operate at top speeds of 25,000 to 30,000 rpm. And you don't want a sharp router bit working its way loose at that speed. Collets are standard in two sizes (corresponding to the diameter of the shafts of router bits) in the United States ($1/4$" [6mm] and $1/2$" [13mm]). In Europe they end up in three metric diameters. Glad I don't have to worry about that!

A base is used to maintain the bit's height above the work. The base is oriented perpendicular to the router bit. There are two general classifications of router, and these are determined by the type of base the router has. One class is fixed-base routers. The bit height on these routers is adjusted prior to use and then locked in at that height during the cut.

The other classification is a plunge router. These routers lower the bit into a cut while running. This is important for making cuts on the inner area of a board. Let's say you're cutting out a window in the wall of your kid's dollhouse. If you tried to do it with a fixed-base router you'd have to rock the router into position while running it, and this can be dangerous and make a mess of your project. Plunge routers make this type of task simpler and safer. They're also great for making signs like the one hanging on some mailboxes.

On plunge routers, the motor assembly rides on two spring-loaded guide bars. The depth can usually be adjusted for very precise depth of cut. These routers excel for inlay and intarsia work and are often just a very nice all-around router.

A question I get all the time is which

type of router is better. The answer is, both. And you can actually afford both these days, but still only buy one router. Most router manufacturers now offer a two- (sometimes three-) base kit that uses one motor. By offering both a fixed and plunge base for a single motor, they've been able to make both router designs accessible to all woodworkers. So you don't have to make a decision. For around $200 you can have both.

Routers are great used as handheld tools, but they also can be mounted in tables (router tables, of course) to allow you to move the wood past the tool rather than the other way around. In general, fixed-base routers are better for use in a router table, but we'll come back to that later.

Power
switch

AC motor

Router body

Base height-
adjusting ring

Quick-release
latch

Base height-
adjusting scale

Knob

Base

Base
plate

Collet

Shaft-locking
button

Router Bit Speed Chart

Bit Size (Diameter)	Max Speed (rpm)
0-1"	24,000
Up to 2"	18,000
Up to 2½"	16,000
Up to 3½"	12,000

Types

Beyond the two styles (plunge and fixed-base), routers also come in three distinct sizes. In the smaller category are trimmers. Originally designed for trimming laminates (Formica), these small routers (with motors ranging from 3.8 to 7.5 amps) are actually very handy, powerful and a pleasure to use for "fine" routing. On top of that, they're the only routers that come with a selection of optional bases for routing on an angle (beveling), in corners (offset base) and with a standard base. And they're pretty inexpensive (usually around $100, moving up to around $150 when you add the bases). The one limitation with trim routers is the collet. These routers are available only with ¼" (6mm) diameter collets limiting the number (and size) of bits they can be paired with.

The router most of us think of when we hear the word is the horse-and-a-half router, available in both fixed- and plunge-base designs. Of course nowadays the manufacturers are messing with the numbers, and these routers are more often called 2 hp routers. It's still the same router, so don't be fooled by the marketing. Most of these motors are rated at around 11 amps and you can't monkey with that statistic, so check the amps, not the horsepower.

These guys are the workhorses of the router world. They get used both in and out of router tables. They're small enough to drag to a job site but also powerful enough to swing a raised panel bit. They often come with both ¼" (6mm) and ½" (13mm) collets and are often available in single-speed or variable-speed configurations. Variable speed is important with this size and larger routers because they have enough torque to handle larger diameter router bits. These larger bits cut best at slower speeds, so variable speed allows the best of both worlds.

Next up on the stand, will you please extend a hand for the "big boys" in the router world, the 3 hp-plus router. These monster routers push the

limits of being called portable power tools. Okay, you can still carry them around, but the torque produced by these larger (15 amp, 3$\frac{1}{4}$ hp) motors can make them hard to control free-hand. They're also heavier, and if you have to move one across wood for 20 minutes at a time your arms are going to start looking like Popeye's. But what a great tool they are for use in a router table! Heck, with one of these things in a table you're almost getting the power and performance of a shaper for significantly less money. (They range in price from around $150 to $300, with most in the $225 range.) These routers also are available in both fixed- and plunge-base configurations, but don't look for too many $\frac{1}{4}$" (6mm) collet versions. That's just silly.

After just a couple of strokes across the sandpaper, the high spots on the base are obvious. Will these high spots keep your router from working? No, but if the base were perfectly flat, it would work better. So we'll fix it.

By moving the router in a simple forward and back motion on the sandpaper (I'm using 220 grit here and that's probably as low a grit as I'd suggest), you can quickly flatten the base of the router.

Maintenance

Routers are also one of my favorite tools because they're very reliable. You can almost always count on your router to be ready to use with little or no maintenance or upkeep. The hardest job is trying to find the wrench and the proper collet. But there are a few things you should do to make sure you get the most out of your router.

There are two items that you should check right out of the box. One is the flatness of the base, and the other is the concentricity of the bit in relation to the base plate. Let's start with the flatness. I'm being a little anal on this and that runs contrary to much of what this book is about. So if you want to skip this part, you'll probably be alright.

The formed plastic base plate on a router is where the tool meets the wood. If there are inconsistencies in the flatness of the base, the router can rock during a cut, and this can affect the look and fit of the cut.

Right when the tool is brand-new, attach the base to the motor (yes, with the motor, because when the base is secured, the clamping action may slightly stress the base shape), then pick a known flat surface. Your workbench or the wing of your table saw should work fine. Lay a piece of fine sandpaper (220 grit or greater) on your flat surface. Then, without lifting or rocking the router, slide the base across the sandpaper a couple of times. Lift up the base and take a look. Chances are you'll find a noticeable number of high spots on the base. To flatten the base, keep stroking. You don't have to end with a completely flat base, but better than two-thirds flat is a good idea.

This sanding process also helps the router after a certain number of hours of use. The base can become scratched or gouged during use. Usually a router is being used on a piece of wood before any sanding is done, so there's not a huge concern about scratching. However, there are occasions to run a router on a finished project, and a gouge in a baseplate can cause catching as the gouge crosses the wood. This can, once again, lead to a less-than-perfect finish on the cut.

So, it's a very simple process to flatten the base. You've already found a flat surface, so all you need to do is keep applying the elbow grease. Keep the router flat on the surface, and try not to rock the router up on an edge of the base. After a fair number of strokes you should be able to see significant progress.

The other thing to check before using a router is the bit concentricity to the base plate. The what-to-who? Simply it's checking to see if the base plate is aligned perfectly centered on the collet. Why is this important? Well, in a perfect world it wouldn't be, but when using a router, about half the time you're using the base plate to guide the cut. If the plate isn't centered on the collet and you don't reference off the same place on the base plate for each cut, you can end up with varying cuts because the distance from the bit to the edge of the plate will vary. Some routers solve this problem by designing flat edges into the base plate that work well to assure no variation affects the cut. Other routers actually come with a concentricity template to help you align the base.

These concentricity templates are usually cone-shaped and slip into the collet. By lowering the loosened base over the template, the cone will center the opening. Then the base is tightened and is accurately centered. But you don't have to have a concentricity template. By using a template guide and the matching diameter bit, you can center your own base.

Collets

As mentioned, collets come in a couple of sizes and the design can vary, but they operate similarly. One recent change in collets that causes some confusion is a locking/self-releasing feature. These collets are designed to

Check your progress periodically. The whole base doesn't have to show scratch marks from the sandpaper. Just hit about 90 percent and you'll be in good shape. After sanding, a little lubricant or polish wiped on the base will smooth away the wear even more.

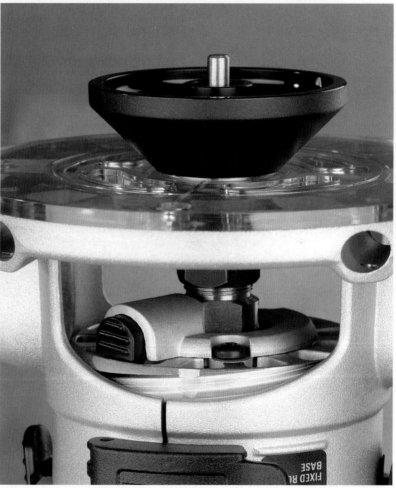

This little jig makes so much sense I don't know why it took them so long to come up with it. The cone, attached to a spindle, is slipped into the collet. Then, with the base plate loosened, the base is moved to snug up against the cone. Then you just tighten down the base, and you should be able to guide the router using any edge of the base without affecting the profile. Slick.

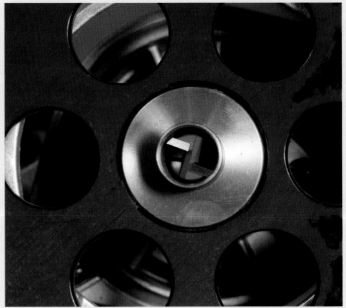

Most routers don't come with a set of template guides (the brass things in this shot). But they do usually have a base with a center hole that's designed to accommodate the guides. They're not expensive ($20 for a set), and you'll find a bunch of ways to use them to increase your router's uses.

One of the uses of template guides (though not one they were designed for) is as a concentricity guide. If you don't have one of the cones, you can fit a matching template guide and straight router bit and nearly perfectly center your base plate by sight.

Just a few passes over an abrasive pad will knock down the tiny burrs that can muck up a router bit shank. It doesn't take much to affect the fit in a tight-tolerance collet.

hold the bit tightly even though the nut has been loosened. This keeps the bit from falling out on the floor and keeps you from overtightening the nut. But if you're not aware of the "feature" you may think the bit is stuck. You need to continue loosening the nut with the wrench until you feel the collet release the bit.

Another piece of collet information — not all bits are built the same and the tolerances between bit and collet are really tight. So if the bit is slightly oversized or undersized (we're talking thousandths of an inch) the bit may slip into the collet easily or too tightly. The loose fit shouldn't be a problem once the nut is tightened. If the bit seems too tight, remove the collet from the router and push the bit in, then replace the collet and bit in the router. While we're talking router bits, they can use a little maintenance themselves. Don't hesitate to take a couple of swipes with an abrasive pad on the shaft of a bit. This will keep dirt, grease and scratches off the bit and help it slip into the collet more easily.

If your router has the option of $1/4$" (6mm) and $1/2$" (13mm) collets, they may be either two separate collets, or the collets may fit into a single interchangeable nut. Word to the wise, keep the loose (not in use) pieces in a safe place. There's nothing more annoying than losing the collet that you need. General maintenance on these little guys isn't too tough. Basically you want to keep the dust off the collet and check the interior as well. Use a toothbrush to keep things clean. You don't want to scratch the interior of the collet because this may affect its ability to hold the bit efficiently. You should also check the interior of the collet for scratches or burrs occasionally. These too can affect the collet's ability to hold a bit. If you do have a burr, you need to sand it down carefully.

Brushes

You won't have access to the brushes on all routers. But first let's talk about the brushes. They aren't brushes. Actually, they're carbon blocks. These blocks are the conductors of the elec-

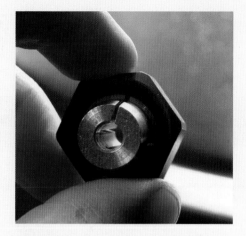

Just like the shank of the bit, take a peek inside your collet for signs of burrs or scratches, and, of course, for dust and built-up pitch. A few seconds of cleaning will stop you from fighting with the bit and collet.

trical current to the commutator that makes the motor spin. Let's just say they're important to the process, and they wear down over time. If your router motor allows access to the brushes, the manufacturer either feels reasonably confident that the router

The brushes are usually hidden behind a cap like the one shown here. A simple screwdriver will remove the cap... but hang on to it! There's a spring behind there.

Once the cap is released, it will push itself out a short distance. The carbon block — that is, the brush — is attached to a spring, wire and metal disc that snugs behind the cap. Pull out the brush, paying attention to how it was seated in the space.

With the brush removed, you can see how much of the carbon block has been worn away and whether it's wearing evenly. This one still has lots of life left. When you replace the brush, it will fit only one of two ways. You can turn the orientation of the block without any harm to the router so don't sweat that. Getting the cap back on the spring is a different matter and takes a certain amount of dexterity.

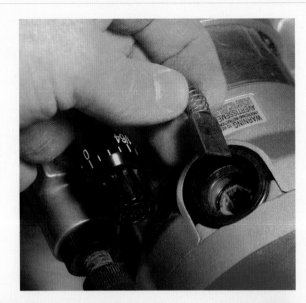

When you're adjusting the base height (this can be either by slipping the motor up or down in the base or by spinning the motor), the latching buckle should be in the open position.

When the height is correct, simply snap the buckle shut. This sure beats the older-style thumb screw that was an industry standard for way too long.

will last long enough to need replacement brushes, or they're very clever at marketing. Anyway, the brushes really don't need to be checked very often — maybe once a year. If the brushes are less than 1/4" (6mm) it's time to put new ones in. This process can be a little tricky, so check the photos on this page and the previous page for some help.

Bases

Bases are also pretty easy to take care of. Basic cleaning and lubricating will handle most of it. Fixed bases are the simplest. The fit to the motor housing is the primary concern. If dust or dirt get into this fit, the base will not fit at all or slip. Get the toothbrush and keep things clean. To keep them moving easily, a little silicone spray will help. Some routers will allow adjustment of the locking mechanism. This can be a subtle adjustment, so spend a few seconds getting it just right. You shouldn't have to force the mechanism closed, but you should get a solid feel to the closure.

Plunge bases have the same cleaning and lubricating concerns as a fixed base, but you also need to clean and lubricate the plunge columns. Same tools here — toothbrush and silicone.

Cords

As with all corded tools, a quick inspection every now and then to make sure the cord isn't cracked or split will avoid electrical problems. Again, not a big deal, but worth mentioning.

A tool that I find handy in my shop is a toothbrush. In fact a battery powered toothbrush makes it easy to clean areas on tools that are hard to reach, like the columns on this plunge router.

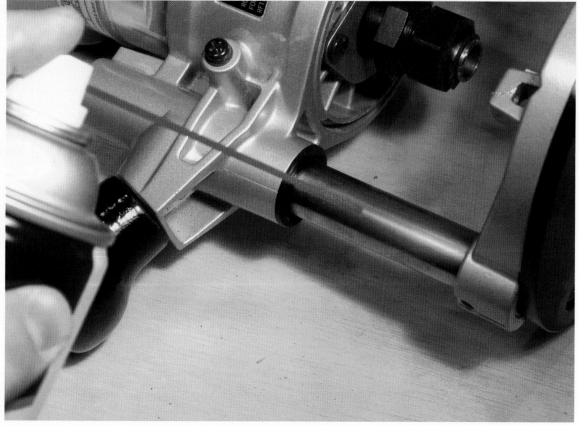

Once everything is cleaned off, it's a good idea to add some lubricant to the columns. A spray lubricant (WD-40 or similar product) is a good choice. Spray it on the columns, then wipe off any excess.

jigsaws

JIGSAWS ARE LIKE POCKETKNIVES for a woodworker. You don't think about pocketknives as a tool very often, but just like a pocketknife, you pull out a jigsaw all the time for a variety of uses. It's a great tool for cutting thin plywood, 2"-thick (51mm) solid oak, aluminum, PVC and even concrete board. Just switch the blade for whatever the application.

And the modern jigsaw is almost always equipped with orbital action that allows you to cut quick and rough or a little slower and with clean finesse. It's portable, corded or battery-powered, easy to handle and nearly maintenance-free. It can cut straight lines like a circular saw (though perhaps not as precisely) as well as circles and complicated interior and exterior curved shapes. Jigsaws can also cut complicated compound shapes by angling the base plate, or shoe. They're very versatile tools.

Another thing that makes jigsaws easy to use is they're actually very safe. Jigsaw blades move up and down only about $\frac{3}{4}$" (19mm) to 1" (25mm) per stroke. It isn't a continuous cutting motion like that of a band saw. Also, the blade will contact the material being cut only as fast as you push the tool. Because of these things contact with the user (your hand) will hurt and leave a mark, but you'd have to work really hard to cause any permanent damage. In fact, you stand more of a chance of burning yourself trying to remove a hot jigsaw blade than actually cutting yourself. Yes, that was a subtle hint about being safe when removing a blade!

Types

The jigsaw is a very simple tool. It's a straightforward universal motor (power ranges from 3.6 amp to 6.4 amp) that spins an eccentric gear. This gear drives the blade holder shaft up and down. Simple. Well, there's a little more to it than that, but it's really all that's necessary to understand the tool. You can buy a jigsaw for as little as $30 or as much as $250. The average price for a saw that you'll appreciate and keep for a while is in the $150 range.

The body of the saw is usually plastic, with the gear housing at the front of the saw in a metal body. The other parts of a jigsaw are the base plate, or shoe, and the blade holder and guide. The shoe is commonly a very simple metal plate that serves as a rest for the tool as the blade cuts. The blade holder and guide will vary by manufacturer, but thankfully, over the past decade, inserting and removing a blade has almost universally become a tool-free operation. (About time!)

Jigsaws are available in two physical versions, but they're still essentially the same mechanical tool. They are either top handle or barrel grip in design. The top-handle design is essentially a barrel grip with a handle grafted to the top of the motor. With the top-handle design, the power switch moves up into the handle, rather than being mounted on the barrel-shaped motor housing. Both styles are popular, and choosing which model is best for you will be a personal preference. I personally enjoy the feel of the barrel-grip design because it has a lower center of gravity and feels more controllable during turns.

How They Work

The blades in jigsaws are designed to cut on the up-stroke. This works well because when the saw (or more accurately, the shoe of the saw) is placed against the wood, the wood is pulled against the shoe as the blade cuts up. This configuration adds stability to the cut. The up-and-down motion of the blade is not actually all that dramatic, usually traveling no more than 1" (25mm). But with the option of variable speed in most models (either controlled by pressure on the trigger or with an independent speed control), jigsaws will operate between 500 and 3,000 strokes per minute. Plenty fast, and easy to control.

Along with variable speed, another feature I mentioned earlier is the orbital action. This is actually pretty cool. The blade can travel simply straight up-and-down, which will provide a smooth, basic cut. Orbital jigsaws usually offer three alternative positions, each pushing the blade slightly forward during the up cut, then returning to a straight downward motion for the return. This action produces a more aggressive cut, with each progressive step being more aggressive. Because of this, the blade cuts faster, but also less cleanly, leaving a rough edge on the cut.

The Parts

Another switch that is found on many jigsaws is for the blower. By channeling the air created by the fan motor in the saw, a blower is added that provides a stream of air directed at the point of the cut. In many jigsaws this feature can be switched on or off. The blower is designed to blow the sawdust out of the way so you can see where you're cutting. Though a clever idea, many of these blowers aren't powerful enough to keep up with the dust.

A related idea that often falls short of actually working on jigsaws is dust collection. A number of jigsaws offer a hollow wand attachment that fits into the shoe and is designed to hook to a shop vacuum and pull the dust away from the cutting area. Usually the area isn't enclosed well enough to create a decent vacuum to adequately remove the dust.

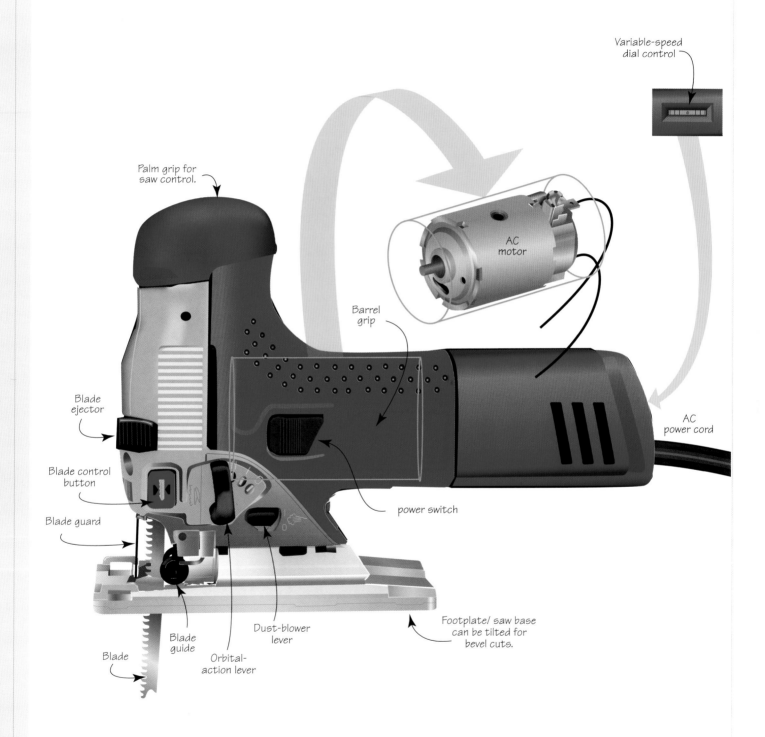

Variable-speed
dial control

Palm grip for
saw control.

AC
motor

Barrel
grip

Blade
ejector

AC
power cord

Blade control
button

Blade guard

power switch

Blade
guide

Dust-blower
lever

Footplate/ saw base
can be tilted for
bevel cuts.

Blade

Orbital-
action lever

The switch on the left of the machine is the orbital control. The zero setting is for no forward orbital action. The blade will move straight up and down for a very clean cut. Positions 1 through 3 will provide an increasingly aggressive cut.

The switch shown here on the right side of the jigsaw is the blower control. On this Milwaukee model you have the option of controlling the amount of air provided by the blower, not just turning it on or off.

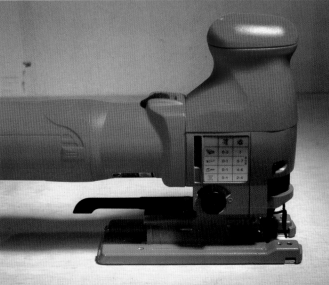

Shown here, the shoe is kicked 45° to the right. Not your standard cut, but possible. The black handle is the tool-free lever release for the shoe — a very handy feature.

It's my experience that the annoyance of fighting with the vacuum hose isn't worth the dust-collection benefit.

Most shoes on jigsaws can be beveled in either one or both directions to form a 45° angle to the blade. This is handy for some operations, but honestly, most jigsaw shoes stay locked at 0° and never move. That said, when you do need to move the shoe, it may require a wrench or screwdriver. Some jigsaws offer tool-free shoe adjustment, and this is a preferable convenience.

Choosing a jigsaw can be tricky. They all look very similar, and what makes one a better choice than the next is commonly inside and therefore not easy to spot. First off, as with most power tools, take a look at the motor. The amp range mentioned earlier is significant. From 3.6 to 6.4 amps is quite a spread. Should you automatically buy the most powerful saw? No. Power is nice but not always necessary. A 5-amp saw is probably adequate power for most tasks. More important, you should consider ease of use and comfort. Ease of use really boils down to how easy it is to change the blade and if the switch is located conveniently. Comfort is how it feels in your hand and how much vibration is in the tool. The last, unfortunately, is a little harder to determine in the store.

Let's take a look at the blade guides and the blade-changing systems. The blade guides on a jigsaw come in a variety of proprietary designs. All support the blade from behind and often from the side, but the amount of side support varies. Jigsaws are prone to wandering in a cut if not properly guided. The blade can start to flex out of square in relation to the shoe, which will create a beveled cut — not what you're usually trying for. The blade guides help control the blade in the cut and reduce this flexing. Most rear blade supports are bearings of some sort that will move with the up-and-down motion of the blade. The side supports may be solid guides, separate bearing

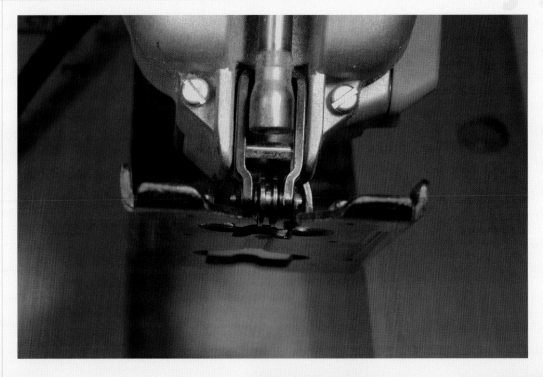

The wheel you see with the groove down the center is the blade guide. The groove keeps the blade supported at the rear as well as guides the blade from both sides. The groove on this Bosch model is only deep enough ($\frac{1}{8}$" [3mm]) to support the blade partially. Other jigsaws may use guides that support the full width of the blade right up to the teeth.

guides, or an integral part of the rear support. Most are like the wheel of a car without the tire on, so it creates a channel in which the blade will track.

The mechanism for changing a jigsaw blade has changed significantly over the past few years but none too soon. Older, or less expensive, jigsaws will require a screwdriver to release a screw that clamps the blade in place in the holder. This makes for slower blade changes, and you end up having to chase a tool to make the change. The great majority of jigsaws today are using toolless blade-changing mechanisms. Most are some variant of a spring-loaded lever at the front of the tool that, when shifted, opens the locking clamp on the blade and allows it to drop free. Some of these mechanisms will require that the blade be turned sideways to be released, even after the lever has been shifted. Others (the ones I enjoy) will actually eject the blade from the holder. Besides being fun, this action keeps your hands cool. Jigsaw blades get hot during use, and you don't want to grab a hot blade to wrestle it out of the holder.

Bosch not only employs a grooved guide wheel but also has a set of blocks that can be engaged against each side of the blade for even greater support. This precision guide system can then be released for less precise cutting needs.

Maintenance

Jigsaw maintenance is simple. Most jigsaws don't even include replaceable brushes to worry about. This isn't a deficit because the action of a jigsaw is usually of short duration and a set of brushes will likely last the life of the tool. If necessary (unlikely) you can always remove the motor housing to access the brushes.

The most important maintenance procedure is to keep things clean. Even with a blower and dust-collection hookup (which I mentioned don't work all that well) things get dusty. And not just dusty — because moving parts, grease and oil are involved to keep things moving smoothly and these attract dust like a magnet. A good toothbrush goes a long way toward keeping the blade-guide mechanism clean and free from dust buildup. Without a good cleaning every now and then the guides can allow that blade to wander off track, adversely affecting the cut.

You also want to keep the shoe in decent shape. If the shoe is bent (due to dropping… yes, we've all done it) the angle of the cut can be thrown off. The surface of the shoe is important as well. If it gets scratched or gouged, sharp edges can be formed and these can quickly scratch up the surface of the wood you're cutting. In fact, a number of manufacturers provide a plastic shoe cover to be used when you're cutting materials that are more susceptible to scratching, such as already finished wood or plastics. A little bit of fine sandpaper or a synthetic pad will help knock down any sharp edges. But keep the plastic shoe cover handy as well.

Another accessory that most jigsaws are sold with is a zero-clearance insert plate. This small plastic piece slips into a space in the shoe and allows just the width of the blade to pass through. This helps reduce tear-out while cutting, which, by the way, is always on the top surface of the wood due to the cutting action, so you should always cut from the backside of your piece to keep the tear-out less visible. While these zero-clearance plates are useful, they're also prone to getting destroyed if a blade is flexed too aggressively during a cut. Consequently, they "disappear" fairly frequently. I'd suggest removing this plate and putting it away for when you really need it.

One other thing to check on corded jigsaws is the cord itself. Probably more than any other corded tool, jigsaws are susceptible to having the cord in the way of the cut… and many a cord has become the unwitting subject of its own tool's aggression. Metabo and Ridgid make jigsaws with removable cords just in case of this unfortunate accident. So it's a good idea to check the cord periodically for cuts, nicks or cracked sheathing. Exposed wires are not a good thing.

The other option to cords is, of course, cordless models. Cordless jigsaws are good options in today's tool market. They're available in a variety of voltages ranging from 12- to 28-volt. As you might expect, the higher the voltage, the more "corded-like"

This blade release is very simple. The lever is simply pushed to one side and the clamps release the blade. This particular model still requires the blade to be turned 90° even after the clamps have been released. Better than some, but other models actually eject the blade, avoiding burned hands.

the cutting performance. Jigsaws are a good application for cordless cutting. Because the action is of short duration and short motion, batteries can last quite a while. Initially, these saws were hampered by low torque and were more a novelty than a useful tool. But today's battery technology allows cordless jigsaws to have impressive torque and capabilities.

As with all battery-powered tools, maintaining the battery is your most important task. Make sure to read the manufacturer's recommendations on extending the battery life. This may include removing the battery from the charger after charging. It may also include completely expending the battery during the first few uses and then fully recharging. Also, batteries don't fare well in extreme heat or cold. So use your head and read the instructions.

That's about it for the jigsaw. Enjoy it. It's a very versatile, convenient and easy-to-care for power tool.

When inserting a blade and allowing the clamps to grab the blade, the clamps should grab the blade squarely.

But if you aren't paying attention, it's possible that the clamps can grab and lock the blade at an angle. This will produce a very poor cut.

There aren't too many areas on a jigsaw to worry about cleaning, but the guides and the blade clamp area are two important ones. I like a toothbrush for getting in these areas, and an inexpensive battery-powered brush makes the cleaning even easier. Buy a new one. They don't taste very good after cleaning off greasy dust.

The black shoe cover shown here is all too often tossed away as soon as the saw is taken out of the box. Worse, the saw may be used with the shoe in place all the time, causing scratches and damage that will defeat the smooth, protective nature of the shoe cover. Put it someplace safe until you need to cut on an easily scratched surface.

drills

LET'S SEE, WHERE TO START with the most popular power tool sold today? As a woodworker you probably own at least one corded and one cordless drill. Most woodworkers I know have more than one cordless drill. And why not? They're incredibly efficient, reasonably affordable and actually offer more features than traditional corded drills. Oh, and they're remarkably maintenance-free! You gotta like that.

My personal goal is to own enough cordless drills that I can leave my most-used drill bits and screw tips in the drills and never have to change them out. I think six should do nicely. Hey, only one more to go! I know what you're thinking: What will he do with all those plastic drill cases? Throw them away! Let me share a little secret with you that I learned from a reader years ago. Old tennis shoes make great drill holders. Simply screw the heel of an old tennis shoe to your shop wall (catch a stud!), then slip the drill into the shoe. It's like a holster ready for the quick draw. And the holsters are adjustable!

Loosen or tighten the laces as necessary to best fit the drill. Want to leave a long $^{3}/_{16}$" (5mm) bit in the drill? No problem — just drill a hole through the toe of the shoe. Sure, it looks a little funny, and your friends may mock you the first time they see it. But they're going to go home and look for old tennis shoes to add to their shop. Bet on it!

But I'm getting a little off topic. Drills can be broken into two large classes: corded and cordless. Although cordless drills continue to gain ground on corded drills for power and duration, I still say everyone needs a corded drill. For those times when you need to put down a deck surface or drill a half-dozen 2" (51mm) holes through wall studs, nothing quite cuts it like a corded drill. Both corded and cordless drills are most commonly available with reversing motors, so you can put a screw in and take it out.

When choosing a drill for yourself, you need to consider how you will use the drill and also how the drill will feel in your hand with extended use. The difference in size between the 12-volt and 18-volt drills shown here is obvious. And the weight difference is just as noticeable.

All-metal chucks are usually a sign of extended durability, but that's not all you should look for in a chuck. Notice the opening of the chuck on each of these drills in the fully closed position. If you're working with very small drill bits, it's possible the drill on the left won't close tight enough on the bit to hold it.

Types

Within the corded drill category re only a few major options to consider. They're available with either a $^3/_8$" (10mm) or $^1/_2$" (13mm) chuck. Usually the $^1/_2$" (13mm) chuck models have higher amperage motors, which means they can handle the larger bits. So, if you're following my logic, the *one* corded drill you should own is one with a $^1/_2$" (13mm) chuck. Get one with a nice long cord and that's about all you need to worry about. I take that back. Should you be faced with the option of a corded drill with either a keyless or keyed chuck, take the keyless. There is an argument that keyless chucks don't have the clamping pressure to adequately hold a large bit under torque. But many of today's keyless chucks also offer a ratcheting lock that adds extra pressure and will hold whatever you need. In fact, it's getting hard to find a drill that still requires a key. And I'm happy about that! Corded drills range in price from under $50 (good for the very occasional woodworker) on up to around $140, with lots of options in between. For a $^1/_2$" (13mm) variable-speed, reversible corded drill, expect to spend around $110.

When it comes to cordless drills, the choices are many. Ranging from 7.2 volts on up to an amazing 28 volts from Milwaukee, there's a power platform for every use. In general I find a 12-volt drill has the juice that I need for most woodworking and around-the-house tasks. If you've got the chance to add a second drill to your collection, then a 14.4- or 18-volt makes sense for the more heavy-duty operations.

Cordless drills range in price from $60 to over $400. For a good cordless drill, plan on spending around $140, though some of the bargain drills are more than adequate for all but the serious woodworker.

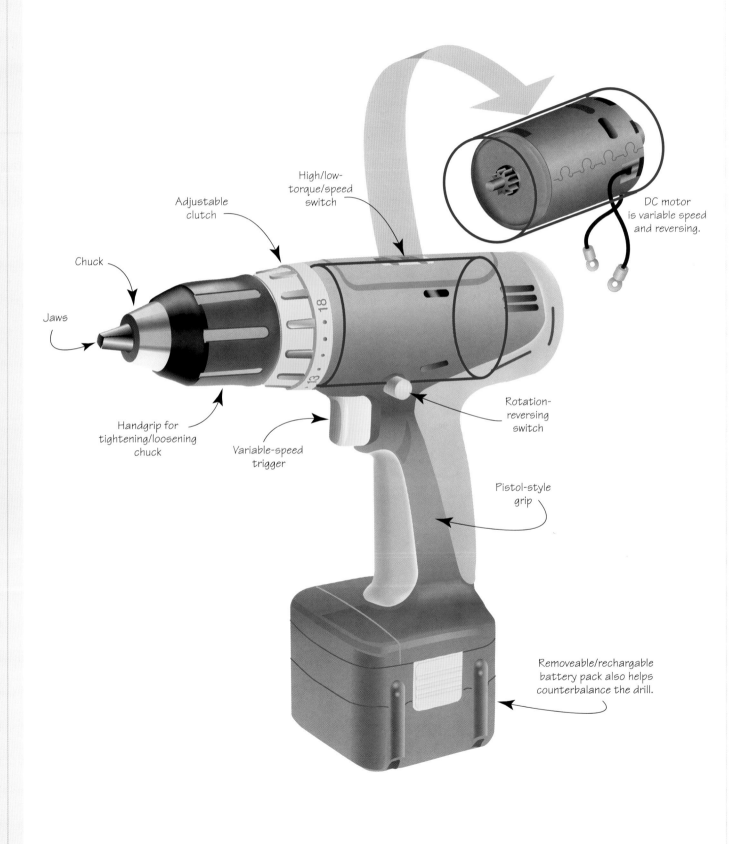

High/low-
torque/speed
switch

Adjustable
clutch

Chuck

Jaws

DC motor
is variable speed
and reversing.

18

13

Rotation-
reversing
switch

Handgrip for
tightening/loosening
chuck

Variable-speed
trigger

Pistol-style
grip

Removeable/rechargable
battery pack also helps
counterbalance the drill.

Parts

There are lots of features available on cordless drills, starting with two motor speeds, which also relates to two torque settings that make cordless drills — drill/drivers. At lower speeds the drills are geared to produce more torque. This is a good setting for putting screws in (driver mode). To drill holes, you need more speed to drill efficiently, but you don't need a great deal of torque. That's what the higher speed setting is for. Simple.

Along with an almost universally available keyless chuck, cordless drills offer clutch settings (from 4 to 24) that allow you to set the drill to stop applying torque when you reach a certain point. This is great for setting brass screws without stripping off the head. Though I think 24 positions might be overkill, I definitely recommend you take advantage of the clutch settings.

There are also some shopping considerations with cordless drills related to their charges, but I'm going to wait until we talk about the maintenance of the batteries to explain the pros and cons in that area.

There aren't a whole lot of safety concerns when using a drill, beyond the obvious of not putting holes in things you shouldn't… like your hand. If you're using a higher-powered drill there is a concern of hurting your wrist if the bit catches in a hole and the drill continues to turn. That's why larger drills are sold with an auxiliary handle that allows convenient two-hand use. Use the handle and avoid an accident.

A couple of quick comments about using a drill. As mentioned, it's a very simple tool. Use the right setting for the task and make sure that your bit or screw tip is tightly secured in the drill. One of the things that throws off some users is being able to drill a straight hole. One technique that I've found useful is grasping the drill with your index finger pointing along the side of the drill, in line with the bit. This requires you to use your middle finger to pull the trigger, but the human body amazingly has a memory for pointing. When you point your index finger straight, the drill bit will follow. Try it. You'll be surprised at how effective it is.

Maintenance

Okay, maintenance. As mentioned, there isn't a whole lot to concern yourself with. Keeping it clean is about your only concern. A general cleanup every so often will add extra life to your drill. You can use an air compressor to blow out the interior workings of your drill by blowing through the air vents. But a better method is to open the drill housing and be more selective about cleaning out the innards. Opening the housing isn't tough, and it's also a good way to get acquainted with your drill. This may be valuable later. A set of screws are all that stands between you and the inside of your drill, but pull the battery or the plug before you start taking things apart.

Two things that can be easily and affordably replaced (should they fail or wear out) are the brushes and the switch. Now, there's a school of thought these days that many of these drills are disposable. This becomes especially prominent when you consider the cost

Besides considering size in respect to your hand, also consider size as it relates to your task. Once again comparing a 12-volt (left) and 18-volt drill, which one is better suited to drilling between wall studs? The power of the 18-volt may be appealing, but if you can't get into the workspace, it's no good. Also notice the clutch and speed settings available on these two cordless drills.

of replacing the batteries (which is the first thing that's going to wear out). A new battery can cost $50. And if you've purchased a midpriced drill with two batteries for under $100, replacing those batteries just doesn't make sense. You can buy a brand-new drill for less. Because of this philosophy, you won't find as many manufacturers offering replaceable brushes. That's okay, because you should get decent life out of the first brushes in relation to the battery life. On corded drills, you're more likely to find replaceable brushes.

Check the brushes for obvious wear and replace if necessary. As for the switch, this is, again, something that shouldn't be a problem. But it is the physical part of the drill that sees the most "action." I've replaced a number of switches over the years, and it's usually a good investment in a drill you enjoy using. Changing out the switch is as simple as disconnecting two electrical leads and plugging in the new one.

One maintenance feature specific to corded drills is checking the cord itself. Look for cracks, cuts or splits in the

The interior of a corded drill is very similar to that of a cordless. Maintenance on these drills is as carefree as the cordless and with less to understand about battery maintenance.

cord. Not only can they stop the drill from running, they can give you quite a shock.

Something else both corded and cordless drills share is a chuck. They come in various designs (most without keys, thank you), can be one- or two-sleeve in design (requiring either one hand, or two, to tighten — I like the one-hand versions) and can be all metal or partially plastic. The jaws

themselves will always be metal, and I encourage you to pay attention to how those jaws close when making a purchase. Maintenance on the chucks is also simple. Again, keep them clean. Your drill should really require no lubrication on the chuck to keep it working fine. This is pretty easy, isn't it?

Now, about those batteries…. This is a complicated subject, made more so by sketchy information from manu-

Wood Screw Pilot Hole Diameters (FOR DRILLS)

Hardwoods

SCREW SIZE	BIT DIAMETER (IN INCHES)
No. 0, No. 1	$3/64$"
No. 2, No. 3	$1/16$"
No. 4, No. 5	$5/64$"
No. 6, No. 7	$3/32$"
No. 8	$7/64$"
No. 9, No. 10, No. 11	$1/8$"

Softwoods

SCREW SIZE	BIT DIAMETER (IN INCHES)
No. 0, No. 1	$1/32$"
No. 2, No. 3, No. 4	$3/64$"
No. 5, No. 6, No. 7	$1/16$"
No. 8, No. 9	$5/64$"
No. 10, No. 11, No. 12	$3/32$"

facturers over the years. Three types of battery chemistries are available in the cordless drill market to date: nickel cadmium, nickel metal hydride and the newest, lithium ion. Nickel cadmium (NiCad) has been around since the first cordless drill and continues to be a reliable and affordable battery platform with good performance curves. Nickel metal hydride (NiMH) is a newer platform (about 10 years old) that manufacturers tout as having longer runtime and better torque for the size of the cells. They're also more environmentally friendly (always dispose of battery cells responsibly — the chemicals in the battery can leach into ground-water systems). NiMH batteries are also a bit more expensive. In my experience, there is some advantage to the NiMH batteries, but if I were getting a good deal on a NiCad drill, I wouldn't change my mind because of the bat-

tery platform. With quick chargers and two batteries per drill, it's not that big a concern.

The newest thing on the market is the lithium ion platform. This battery technology has been around for a while in cell phones. It offers great runtime, but always had a problem with energy drain. Essentially, making a phone call was a reasonable energy drain for these batteries, but to drill a 1" (25mm) hole in oak with a spade bit was too taxing on this battery and it couldn't keep up. New chemistries have, apparently, solved this problem. The platform is currently available in a 28-volt system that is sized similarly to a 14.4-volt drill, with significantly improved performance. Of course, remember the $400 drill I mentioned… yep, that's where this one is price today. The future looks good for cordless drills.

But beyond the batteries — and

more important, where you can make a difference in the life of your drill — is the battery charger and how the batteries need to be maintained. Depending on the manufacturer, you can get a 3-hour, 1-hour or 20-minute charger for your drill. As you might expect, price will play a factor in which you get. Most drills today are sold with two batteries, but most also come with a single charger. Not a great difficulty, but the more feature-laden kits are now offering dual chargers.

Let's address (and simplify) one of the largest charger problems — how to charge. First off, battery memory. The common belief continues that if a new battery isn't charged fully on its first charge, it will never take a full charge. Not true, you can bring a battery back to full charge, but it's still better to start the battery off correctly. Most manufacturers recommend fully charging and fully draining the battery during the first few uses. Is that so hard? Go ahead and spend the time to give your batteries the best chance at a long and productive life. If you skipped this part to begin with, go ahead and do it anyway. Fully discharge and charge the battery a few times, and the battery will rebound to a good runtime charge.

Now the other taboo. Can you leave the battery in the charger without damaging the battery? Yes, if you have the right type of charger. Chargers are now available with smart, or diagnostic, capabilities that allow you to leave the battery in the charger. As batteries charge, they heat up. To keep the battery from overheating, the chargers have cool-down periods during the charge. If the battery is fully charged and left in the charger, the charge will continue to try to apply a charge, keeping the heat up at a level that's not good for the battery. Smarter chargers now recognize the fully-charged status and actually drop into a maintenance phase that applies a low-level charge to maintain the battery's charge, but doesn't heat up to a point that can damage the battery. How can you tell if you've got a smart charger? Look for "trickle charge" or "diagnostic" information in the charger description. At worst, read the directions! This type of charger will cost a little extra, but in my book, it's probably the most important feature on any cordless tool.

To sum it all up, buy the drill (or drills, heh, heh) that will meet your needs and circumstances. That may be three less expensive drills or one top-of-the-line model. Enjoy it, and keep the battery properly charged (if cordless) and you'll have years of good service from these very low-maintenance tools.

A fairly standard, quality battery charger. The indicator light is simple and the explanation for the light is obvious and clear. Nothing fancy, just the information you need.

Battery-charging technology continues to evolve and improve. This 30-minute charger will charge two batteries simultaneously. The indicator lights are still simple, and the manufacturer has added a couple of other steps so the user can understand the stages the battery goes through during recharging. To make the shorter charge time possible, this charger utilizes internal fans to reduce the heat built up during charging. Also note the holes in the base of the battery. These holes allow air to move past the battery cells, again, improving cooling during each charge.

sanders

FOR AS LONG AS SANDPAPER has been around, there have been woodworkers that dread sanding. When sanding by hand was the only option, this very necessary woodworking task was even more onerous. With the addition of powered sanders, the job has gotten quicker, but it's still not a lot of fun. And don't think you're getting out of hand sanding. It's still necessary for lots of tasks. Sure, I've tried using my random-orbit sander to soften the edges on table tops. More often than not I get an interesting scalloped edge and mess up the pad on the sander. So don't throw away your sheets of sandpaper.

Using the correct sander for the task makes things even easier. A number of sanders are available for woodworkers, from precise detail sanders on up to drum sanders for handling large panels. One of the most useful sanders in a shop is a combination belt/disc sander. This tool actually came out of the metal-working industry, but it's a handy woodworking tool as well. You may use the thing only once a month, but when you do, it's a great time-saver.

But I'm not going to talk about the belt/disc sander here. I'm going to spend your valuable time on the sanders that see the most use in woodworking shops. These are belt sanders and finishing sanders. So let's talk about them.

This is a 3 x 21 belt sander. That designation means the belt is 3" (76mm) wide and 21" (533mm) long. It has all the bells and whistles including variable speed and a slow start motor for easier control.

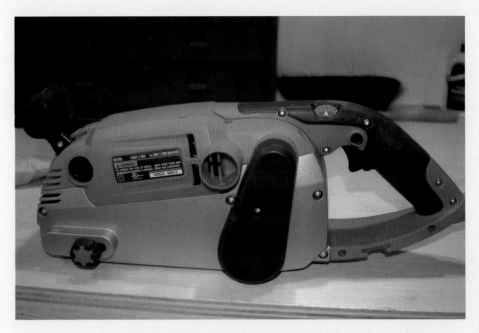

From this angle you can see the variable-speed control, the lock-on switch (handy when you're doing lots of sanding), the tracking control knob and the dust-collection port.

Belt Sander

In my opinion, belt sanders really don't belong in a woodworking shop. They're a very rough tool and can cause more damage than good if you're not familiar with their operation. But, I own one and have used them for decades. There are just some jobs that require the quick removal or leveling of a surface that calls for a belt sander.

The most common belt sanders take 3"-wide (76mm) or 4"-wide (102mm) belts. A 4" (102mm) sander will give you more surface area on the material, making it easier to level a panel, but the extra size also makes them a little harder to control. And it only takes a second to remove too much material with a belt sander. Belt sanders' motors range in size from 5 amps to 12 amps. Again, more power means more to control, and I find the middle of the pack adequate for most woodworking tasks. Pricing will range between $120 to $200, so it's not a tool that you should buy just in case.

Let's look at maintenance on a belt sander first. These machines are built tough to take abuse. Maintenance on them is fairly simple and centers on the belt itself. Because of the way the belt rides on two cylindrical rollers, the rollers need to be in perfect parallel with one another to keep the belt tracking in the center of the rollers. It's much like a band saw — you adjust the tracking each time you put on a new belt.

Removing a belt is the easy part. Simply roll the sander onto its side with the open side of the belt exposed. The flick of a handle releases the spring mechanism and lets the belt slide off the rollers. Once you've got the belt off, it's time to do a little maintenance inspection.

On a belt sander is a part called the platen. The platen is a thin sheet of metal backed most commonly by a sheet of cork. This platen is attached at one end to the underside of the sander and fits between the inside of the sanding belt and the shoe of the sander. Its purpose in life is to provide a flat but slightly springy support, to the belt. It's also the place where the back of the belt rubs, so the platen will wear over time and need replacing.

With the belt removed you can take a look at the platen and inspect it for damage. It should be obvious without removing the platen if the cork is badly damaged, but you may want to take it off every so often to double-check. The platen is also prone to thinning at the unattached end and should be checked periodically. If it's time to replace the platen, it's a quick job and well worth the time.

Putting the belt back on is the tricky part. Well, actually putting the belt on is easy — getting the belt to track correctly takes some finesse. With the tension lever open, check the direction of the belt (yes, there is a correct direction) and just slip the belt over the rollers. With the handle closed you should be able to go right to work, right? Not so. Every belt is slightly different from another. Whether it's slightly longer or shorter, or the seam is at a different angle, all these things add up to make it necessary to readjust the tracking almost every time you put on a new belt.

To change the belt, you need to release the tension handle on the side of the sander. The handle may not be obvious at first because these handles are designed to fit flush against the sander to stay out of the way.

To remove the belt you simply grasp the handle and pull it away from the sander body. This compresses the spring against the front roller allowing it to back away from the belt. There will now be ample room to slip the belt over the rollers.

Belt sanders take a beating because they're not a finesse tool. If it's set down on an awkward surface or a screw or some other tool left on a bench, the platen can be bent, dented or badly scratched. Take a second to check the platen for damage every time you change out a belt.

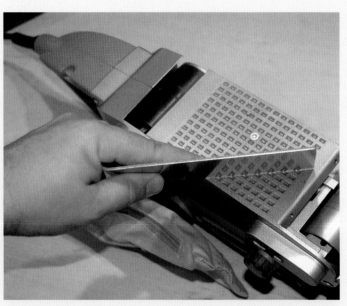

As with a block sander, the cork on the back of a belt sander's platen is the shock absorber. It will wear — that's what it's designed to do. When the cork starts to fall apart, it's time to replace the platen.

Although this platen is new, the most common area for a platen to wear is at the loose, straight end. The metal on the platen will start to thin at that end to a point where the shoe of the belt sander is exposed. You're actually past time to replace it if that happens.

Because of the way the belts are seamed, there is a set direction the belt must fit on the sander for proper performance. The manufacturers conveniently have marked an arrow on the interior of the belt to indicate the direction of travel. See the forward arrows at the top of the belt.

Slide the belt over the rollers and platen and align the outside edge of the belt with the platen, then drop the handle back in place, tightening the belt.

By turning the tracking knob you adjust the angle, or camber, of the front wheel. You're ideally looking for a sweet spot in the center of that tracking range. Camber in (left) will push the belt to the inside of the rollers, whereas camber out (right) will let the belt run off the wheels.

Turning the knob too far clockwise moves the belt up against the interior of the housing. If left in this position, the belt will rub against the housing, destroying both the belt and the housing.

The front roller angles to adjust the tracking, and fine-tuning that tracking will keep the belt running smooth and straight. This is an operation that has to be done with the sander running, so make sure you've either got the sander solidly attached to your bench or that you have a good grip on it. You can set the tracking with the belt facing either up or down, but I like being able to see the belt so I do it upside down.

Ideally, the belt should track in the center of the platen and be centered on the rollers, but each manufacturer has variations. Opt for tracking centered on the wheels for the most reliable performance.

And there you have it, you're ready to sand. As with most woodworking tools, a good spritz of compressed air every now and again to clean out the dust is a good idea. As for extended maintenance concepts, you may need to replace the brushes down the road, and though unlikely, a drive belt could snap. Other than that, check the cord for breaks, and you should have a happy belt-sanding experience... just remember to take it slow!

Turning the knob too far in the other direction moves the belt out extended past the rollers. This isn't a good idea either because there's not support for the belt, and if left tracking to the outside the belt will eventually walk off the rollers entirely.

When you've got the belt centered over the rollers, you're ready to start sanding. Notice that on this sander, part of the platen is still exposed. It's more important to center the belt over the rollers than over the platen.

Of all the portable tools with accessible brushes, I think I've "accessed" more of them on belt sanders. These tools put a drain on a motor like no other, and the brushes tend to wear quicker. Luckily, it's a simple task to pop out both brushes and replace them.

Most likely you won't run into this, but I've had to replace the drive belt on a couple of belt sanders. You'll know when it happens because they're more likely to snap than simply stop grabbing. It's really easy: Just remove the cover and slip the belt over the drive wheels. Slip the new belt in place and align the teeth. Oh, and put the cover back on, please.

Finishing Sanders

Now let's look at the finishing sanders. One of the great things about finishing sanders (beyond the time and energy they save you) is how simple they are to take care of. There really isn't a lot to know about or worry about. Even better, if something really bad happens to your random-orbit sander (like you drop it in your water bucket that you keep by your bench for glue-ups… not that it's likely), they're so affordable that they're almost disposable items. Around $60 will buy you all the sander you really need.

There are, of course, some maintenance items you should do rather than just buy a new one, and those are related to the backing pad for the sandpaper or discs. Both random-orbit sanders and block sanders have pads supporting the paper. Random orbit sanders can use either hook-and-loop or pressure-sensitive adhesive pads, and both will wear over time. In addition, it's always a good idea to keep the dust out of the inner workings of your sander.

If your pad is worn, the part is fairly inexpensive (usually under $20) and takes only a few minutes to replace. If you do have a problem that keeps the sander from running, you can get into the interior, but once again, if it's a two-year-old tool that cost $60, you should just bite the bullet and get a new one.

For the amount of time these tools can save you in the shop, it really is pretty impressive how easy they are to take care of.

A side view of the two most common finishing sanders. The random-orbit sander on the left is designed to leave virtually no sanding marks on the material. The block sander may leave a few marks on the wood, but its square design lets you get into corners where a random-orbit sander can't reach. If you're sanding the inside of a cabinet, those corners will come in handy.

Here's a look at a hook-and-loop pad on a random-orbit sander (left) and a standard pad on a block sander (right). The standard pad works fine on the block sander because there are locking clamps at the front and rear of the pad to hold the paper in place. You can use a standard pad on a random-orbit sander, but the paper you use needs to be self-adhesive, or PSA (pressure-sensitive adhesive) to stick. I'm a strong advocate of the hook-and-loop system because PSA paper can't be reused once removed. And because it's always a good idea to work through a range of sanding grits when finishing a project, you could throw away a lot of PSA paper, or simply reuse the hook-and-loop discs.

Hook-and-loop pads will show damage with time. You'll be able to see sections of the pad where the hooks have broken off or been worn away. When enough of these hooks are damaged your paper won't stay on the pad and it's time to replace it.

Block sander pads wear also. You'll notice cuts in the soft backing material and it may thin or break away on the edges. If the pad starts to erode, you aren't getting proper support on the sanding paper. It's an easy five-minute job to put on a new pad.

Those little plastic hooks can catch more than the loops on the sanding disc. Give 'em a quick air bath to blow things out of the way. For a quick clean you can blow air through the dust-collection holes in the pad to clean out some of the gathered dust in the fan section.

The air vents at the top of this model are where the air is vented from the fan. Dust can build up inside the vents as well. Give them a squirt of air, too.

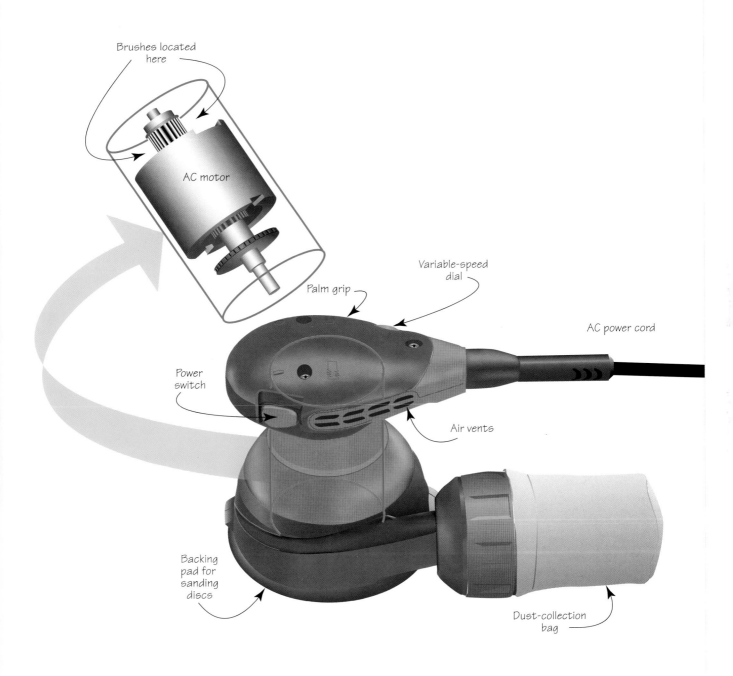

Brushes located here

AC motor

Variable-speed dial

AC power cord

Palm grip

Power switch

Air vents

Backing pad for sanding discs

Dust-collection bag

It takes removing only a few screws to pop the pad off a random-orbit sander. While you're changing the pad, take an extra second to blow out the interior of the sander with some compressed air. Dust is your enemy.

With the pad removed from the block sander, you gain access to the fan and much of the dusty interior. This is also a good place to use your air nozzle to clean things out. Keep an eye on the paper retainer clips stuck on the pad. They can pop off and go missing!

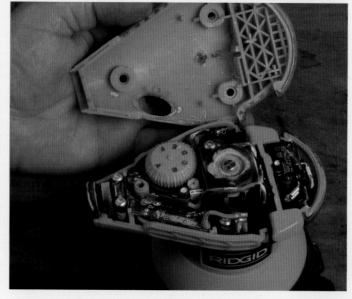

With the top popped on the random-orbit sander you have access to the electronics (leave them alone except to blow out the dust) and the switch, should it ever need replacing.

Sandpaper

No matter what type of sander you're using for your woodworking, it's going to need sandpaper on it to make it work. Just like the tires on your car, selecting the correct type and grit of sandpaper for each task will improve the finished product. This is a lot more important than you might think. If you are the most amazing finisher in the world but you haven't sanded your project properly, it's still going to look like garbage. Finishing starts with a good sanding job, so don't skimp on this step.

There are a couple of things to know about sandpaper. The first is the different types of grit material, or abrasive, used on the sandpaper, and the second is the different grit sizes. Choosing the right abrasive will extend the life of your sandpaper and also speed your sanding (and that's a great thing!).

There are three main abrasive types used by woodworkers. They are: aluminum oxide, garnet, and silicon carbide. Of the three, aluminum oxide gets used more often than garnet or silicon carbide. It's a man-made material that fractures easily. What does this mean? Well, sandpaper is only as efficient as the sharp edges that are exposed on the abrasive material. A new sheet of sandpaper is full of nice, sharp edges. But as you sand, the process itself can soften those sharp edges making the paper less efficient. Because aluminum oxide fractures, or breaks apart easily during use, there are always new sharp edges being exposed to keep the sandpaper working better longer. This means less work for you and less sandpaper to have to buy.

All abrasive materials break down as you use them, and garnet is no exception. Garnet used to be the abrasive of choice before aluminum oxide came around. It's still a decent abrasive material, but as it fractures, the edges left aren't as sharp as those on aluminum oxide granules, so it will wear faster and cut less efficiently. Some woodworkers will use garnet as their final sanding product to reduce concerns of leaving minute sanding marks on the wood. This is a decent idea, but you can also deal with this concern by increasing the grit level of your sandpaper. More on that in a second.

The last abrasive material I want to talk about is silicon carbide. This material is often found on wet/dry sandpaper. Although this paper is used on car finishes, it also works very well on the finish applied to woodworking projects. Silicon carbide papers aren't usually used on bare wood but rather between coats of finish. This could be lacquer finishes or almost any other finishing process.

Sandpaper grits run across a wide range starting around 36 grit on up to 2000 grit. In general, you shouldn't be using either end of this spectrum on your woodworking.

Every woodworker will have his personal preference for the grits used, but there is little argument that working through the grits (from coarse to fine) is a good idea, with a number of stops in the middle. My personal sequence is to never start below 60 grit and use only 60 grit on a belt sander to level a glued-up panel. For projects that don't have a leveling issue, 100 or 120 is a good starting place. These are pieces that might have machining marks on them from the jointer or planer that need to be knocked down.

From 120 I move on to 220 grit and sometimes that's far enough. If you're working with a fine-grained wood, such as maple or cherry, an extra step on up to 320 grit works well for me. Again, you may choose to make more stops along the way or finish at a higher grit. It's a personal thing.

With finishing papers (silicon carbide) 400 grit is all I usually use. There's not the concern of working through a progression of grits because the finish itself is already pretty darn flat. You're just knocking down dust nubs and bumps left by the liquid finish.

Here's an extra bit of information that you should find useful. Sandpaper grit is most commonly marked in one of two different manners. If the sandpaper was manufactured in the United States, it will include only the grit size (220). If it was manufactured to a European standard the markings will have a P in front of the numbers (P220). Of course, it would too much to ask that the numbers would still correspond to the same size abrasive particles. Nope, they had to make it harder. But it's not even as simple as saying there's a 5-percent difference in the sizes. At 180 grit (either with or without a P) the particles are the same size, whether U.S. or European. To either side of 180 is a graduating scale. Below 180 the American grit sizes are about 10 percent smaller; while above 180 the difference increases to the point where the abrasive particle on an American 320 grit abrasive is 36 microns in size, whereas the European equivalent is 46 microns.

This is interesting, but don't get bogged down with it. The grit sizes are close enough that you won't dramatically affect your project by adding a P.

suppliers

BLACK & DECKER
626 Hanover Pike
Hampstead, MD 21074
800-544-6986
www.blackanddecker.com

BOSCH TOOL CORP.
1800 W. Central Rd.
Mount Prospect, IL 60056
877-267-2499
www.boschtools.com

BRIDGEWOOD
Wilke Machinery Company
3230 N. Susquehanna Trail,
York, PA 17402-9716
800-235-2100
www.wilkemachinery.com

CRAFTSMAN
3333 Beverly Rd.
Hoffman Estates, IL 60179
800-349-4358
www.craftsman.com

DELTA MACHINERY
4825 Hwy. 45 N.
P.O. Box 2468
Jackson, TN 38302-2468
800-223-7278
www.deltawoodworking.com

DEWALT INDUSTRIAL TOOL CO.
701 E. Joppa TW425
Baltimore, MD 21286
800-4dewalt
www.dewalt.com

FEIN
1030 Alcon St.
Pittsburgh, PA 15220
800-441-9878
www.feinus.com

GENERAL
835, rue Cherrier
Drummondville (Quebec)
Canada, J2B 5A8
819-472-1161
www.general.ca

GRIZZLY
1821 Valencia St.
Bellingham, WA 98226
800-523-4777
www.grizzly.com

HITACHI
Norcross, GA
800-706-7337
www.hitachipowertools.com

JET WMH TOOL GROUP, INC.
2420 Vantage Dr.
Elgin, IL 60123
800-274-6848
www.jettools.com

MAKITA
14930 Northam St.
La Mirada, CA 90638-5753
800-462-5482
www.makitausa.com

METABO
P.O. Box 2287
1231 Wilson Dr.
West Chester, PA 19380
800-638-2264
www.metabousa.com

MILWAUKEE ELECTRIC TOOL CORP.
13135 W. Lisbon Rd.
Brookfield, WI 53005
800-SAWDUST (729-3878)
www.milwaukeetool.com

PANASONIC
One Panasonic Way
Secaucus, NJ 07094
800-405-0652
www.panasonic.com/consumer_
electronics

PORTER-CABLE CORP.
4825 Hwy. 45 N.
P.O. Box 2468
Jackson, TN 38302-2468
800-321-9443
www.portercable.com

POWERMATIC WMH TOOL GROUP, INC.
2420 Vantage Dr.
Elgin, IL 60123
800-274-6848
www.powermatic.com

RIDGID
400 Clark St.
Elyria, OH 44035-6108
800-4-RIDGID
www.ridgid.com

RYOBI TECHNOLOGIES, INC.
1428 Pearman Dairy Rd.
Anderson, SC 29625
800-323-4615
www.ryobitools.com

WOODSTOCK INTERNATIONAL, INC.
P.O. Box 2309
Bellingham, WA 98227-2309
800-840-8420
www.woodstockinternational.
com

WOODTEK
Woodworker's Supply
5604 Alameda Place NE
Albuquerque, NM 87113
800-645-9292
www.woodworker.com

index

More Great Titles from Popular Woodworking Books!

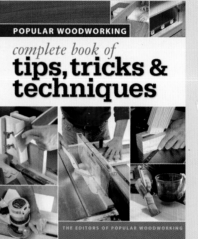

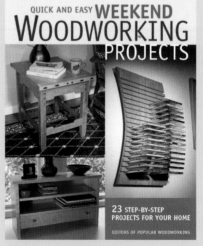